Paperweights
of the
19th & 20th Centuries

A Collector's Guide

Paperweights
of the
19th & 20th Centuries

A Collector's Guide

Anne Metcalfe

MILLER'S PAPERWEIGHTS OF THE 19TH & 20TH CENTURIES:
A COLLECTOR'S GUIDE
by Anne Metcalfe

First published in Great Britain in 2000 by Miller's, a division of
Mitchell Beazley, imprints of Octopus Publishing Group Ltd,
2–4 Heron Quays, London E14 4JP

Miller's is a registered trademark of Octopus Publishing Group Ltd

Commissioning Editor **Anna Sanderson**
Executive Art Editor **Vivienne Brar**
Editors **Emily Anderson & Claire Musters**
Designer **Louise Griffiths**
Indexer **Sue Farr**
Picture Research **Lois Charlton & Maria Gibbs**
Production **Jessame Emms**
Specially commissioned photography **Steve Tanner**
Jacket photography **Stuart Chorley**

ISBN 1 84000 309 X
A CIP catalogue record for this book is available from the British Library
Set in Bembo, Frutiger and Shannon
Produced by Toppan Printing Co., (HK) Ltd.
Printed and bound in China

Jacket (from bottom left clockwise): Antique St Louis double clematis,
£1,600–1,800/$2,550–2,875; Perthshire swirl, c.£250/$400; Ken
Rosenfeld crystal egg weight, c.£350/$550; Paul Ysart half-spoke pattern,
c.£250/ $400; Clichy spaced millefiori with rose, £600–750/$950–1,200;
Half title page: Paul Ysart aventurine snake, £900–1,150/$1,450–1,850;
Contents page: Venetian silhouette weight, £1,800–2,100/$2,875–3,350

contents

Introduction

Has the beauty of a paperweight ever caught your eye and made you wonder how it was made, and by whom? This book reveals the secrets of identifying paperweights. It is divided up chronologically so that you can find your way round the history of paperweight-making easily. To learn about paperweights you need to get out and about. When you look at a weight, try to use the knowledge you have absorbed from the book. Turn the weight over. Is it frosted? If so, it is likely to be Chinese (and the pages on Chinese weights in this book will provide more clues). A good modern weight should tell you most of its history on the base.

The price you should pay

Consider the price of any weight you wish to purchase. You will have to decide for yourself what factors there are about a paperweight that make it worth more or less than the book guide price. Is it in perfect condition? (The prices given in the book are for perfect weights.) If it is cracked it has little or no value. If it is chipped it may be polishable, but you must decide how bad the damage is and whether it is worth the risk of having the weight repolished.

Where to find paperweights

Auctions are good places to find weights but to get the best out of them you need some expertise. Be aware that you cannot take your goods back if you find a fault or simply change your mind. Those intent on using auction houses should try general sales, where most of the bargains are to be found.

If you wish to build up a fine, specialized collection of weights, then using a dealer is the best way. Tell the dealer what you are looking for and he or she will let you know where to find them. You can also trade-in with dealers: discuss with your dealer what you want to find, or what you have already spotted in their stock, and tell them what you have that you might like to "trade-in" against the more expensive weight in their stock. They will negotiate with you the kind of price they will allow against the weight they are selling. It is then up to you and the dealer to come to an agreement on the deal.

Another very enjoyable way of gaining experience is by visiting antique fairs. Here you will find a range of paperweights and it is fun and instructive to try to identify them. You may discover one that suits both your taste and wallet.

Looking after your own collection

Do spend some time considering how you want to display your collection of weights. Wall cabinets are useful if space is at a premium. Try to avoid placing the weights on a wooden windowsill; the sun has been known to leave a scorch mark beneath the paperweight and the heat may also crack the weight.

To keep your weights in pristine condition they will need to be washed regularly. Be sure to use tepid water and never plunge a cold weight into hot water because it may crack. Also remember to protect your collection financially: insure each item and keep careful records. You should also keep original invoices.

Prices

The prices for antiques vary, depending on the condition of the item and also according to geographical location and market trends.

The price ranges given throughout the book are a general guide to value only. The sterling/dollar conversion is at a rate of £1 = $1.60.

Paperweight techniques: millefiori

Before a millefiori paperweight can be made, the "canes" have to be created. Each one is made by pressing molten glass into a mould, leaving it to cool, removing it, dipping it into more molten glass of a different colour, pressing it in turn into a bigger mould and then repeating the process as many times as desired. When this is finished, the hot glass is stretched by attaching pontil rods (long iron rods) to both ends of the molten glass. The glassmakers hold the pontil rods and pull until the glass becomes very thin. It is then cracked into several lengths and taken away to be cut into cross sections. It is these sections that are called canes and which make up the beautiful millefiori patterns that look so much like a bed of flowers – in fact the Italian word "millefiori" means "a thousand flowers". The canes are often fused together in finer paperweights.

1 A thick, squat mould of molten glass is fixed to a pontil rod and pulled gently until it is very fine.

2 Many pulled rods are bundled together and heated to make one complex cane. They will be cut into slices.

3 The canes are put in a collar to hold them and are then picked up by a piece of clear glass on a pontil rod.

4 The canes are encased in clear glass; the weight is ready to be knocked off the rod into a bucket of sand.

Abstract

The basic procedure for making an abstract paperweight is quite simple. A "gather" of glass is put onto a pontil rod, rolled in some coloured ground glass, turned round on the end of the pontil rod and dipped in the pot of molten glass to get a further layer. A bubble pattern can then be inserted before the glass gather is "marvered". When it is the desired shape it is knocked off the pontil. For these procedures glassmakers need to have a "pot" of glass mixed from sand and various chemicals, the most important of which are potash or soda. Sand constitutes up to 80 per cent of the mix. The finest glass includes a high percentage of lead and is distinguished by the word "crystal". Glassworkers each have their own formula for this, and often will not divulge it. The pictures below are from a series showing Peter Holmes of Selkirk making a magnum weight.

1 A "gather" of glass is about to be dipped in one of several ground glass colours.

2 Long spurs of glass are pulled out to make the beginning of the internal pattern.

3 The paperweight is upended and fixed firmly while more molten glass is added.

4 The resulting weight, when shaped, is knocked off the pontil rod into sand to be cooled.

Lampwork

Lampwork paperweights incorporate a technique that gives spectacular results (see the weights on pp50–51). Many people imagine that the flowers are inserted into the glass but in fact the opposite is true. The flowers are made laboriously, petal by petal, then assembled and finally joined together by careful heating. They become part of a paperweight when the clear molten glass is dropped into place over the top; the flowers have been kept at the right temperature by the metal base plate on which they are assembled. The weight is then built up layer by layer with repeated dipping and shaping. If the lampwork is picked up upside down then it is a simple matter to build up the necessary amount of clear glass around it. Some paperweight makers, however, transfer the weight from one pontil to another in order to work from both sides.

1 These are the various rods for the lampwork. When put together they form the shape of the flowers.

2 The lampworker shapes a delicate single petal from a heated coloured rod.

3 The piece of lampwork is set on the heated base plate, ready to be picked up.

4 When the paperweight is in its molten state the lampwork looks black; as it cools it changes colour.

Venice & Murano

Murano is the glass-making island in the city of Venice and it is thought by some that glass was made there as early as the 13thC. The story in terms of paperweights starts in 1845. It was then that a Venetian took a scrambled paperweight to a trade convention in Vienna, where a French businessman took it home and showed it to glassmakers there. They saw its possibilities and so began the paperweights that we now know. Today's paperweight collectors who visit Murano often come back disappointed, with tales of poor-quality weights. There is some truth to this, but it is also a very rich and fruitful collecting field because among the cheap gift weights can be found some excellent ones. These can be bought for less than their intrinsic value because so few collectors rate Muranese weights highly. Look out for the fine double overlays made by the firm of A.L.T.

▼ **Venetian scrambled weight**
This Venetian scrambled weight is of tremendous historical interest as it is believed to be of the type that was shown at the Vienna Trade Convention. The rare portrait canes depict Italian dignitaries of the time, such as the Pope. The canes are usually laid on their sides, with aventurine sparkling among them. Venetian weights have a characteristically uneven surface; if the surface is smooth it is due to repolishing. The weight is made of soda glass, making it quite light.

Venetian scrambled weight, 1847, diam. 6.5cm/2½in, **£1,800–2,100/$2,875–3,350**

Muranese setter on white ground, post-World War II, diam. 8.25cm/3¼in, **£55–80/$90–125**

◄ **Muranese setter on white ground**
These weights with transfer prints on a white ground are likely to be mistaken by an inexperienced collector as being 19thC, not 20thC. They have even appeared in auction house catalogues as 19thC weights worth £200/$325, and one featuring a Montgolfier Balloon was recently offered for a similar price on the fair circuit. Their subjects are usually animals, but it is the white ground and cane garland that are typical features. This weight was made by the Muranese firm of Ferro & Lazzarini.

Muranese three-dimensional squirrel, post-World War II, diam. 7.5cm/3in, **£65–85/$105–135**

▲ Muranese three-dimensional squirrel

There are many paperweight makers on the island of Murano, most of whom seem to market their work co-operatively under the "Made in Murano" label. The firm of Ferro & Lazzarini are known for making three-dimensional items and this is a good example of their work. Their other favourite subjects include ducks and pears, and the pears also appear in a double-overlaid form. As with other Muranese weights, the base of this squirrel weight is polished flat.

▼ Muranese modern crown weight

Modern Murano crowns are commonly found, especially in Murano itself. This type of weight is called a crown because it bears a resemblance to ceremonial royal crowns. They are generally inexpensive to buy, but of very nice quality and the base is always polished flat. With these weights it is worth looking out for more than two colours in the twists. Muranese crowns do not have a central cane to finish off the centre. The Muranese firm of Fratello Toso made crowns in the 1970s, but they closed in 1978. Crowns are still produced by other Muranese makers, such as Ferro & Lazzarini and AVEM.

Muranese modern crown weight, post-World War II, diam. 7.5cm/3in, **£25–35/$40–55**

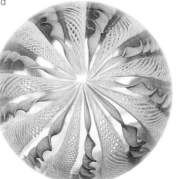

Muranese weights
There is little known about individual makers and it is difficult to identify them by their canes as they also sold them on to others, but the weights listed below are known to be by the firm of Ferro & Lazzarini:
• Canework pictures of houses and trees
• "Zodiac" series – gold leaf motifs

FACT FILE

Muranese cog cane patterned weight, post-World War II, diam. 7cm/2¾in, **£30–50/$50–80**

▲ Muranese cog cane patterned weight

Above all other styles, the cog cane patterned weight is what Murano is best known for. The canes in this picture are almost certainly the work of the firm of Fratelli Toso, a long-established Muranese firm. Cog cane patterns can be poorly executed, but sometimes it is possible to find a weight without any distortion. It is worth buying such a weight, as they are often good value.

Antique Baccarat

Baccarat was established in 1764, when it was known as Verrerie de
Sainte Anne. During the 19thC it changed its name several times, but
it is now known as Compagnie des Cristalleries de Baccarat. The company
started to make paperweights after they were shown the famous Venetian
paperweight made by Pietro Bigaglio. A glassmaker in Venice and Murano
in the 19thC, Bigaglio made the first ever paperweight to be shown at
the Vienna Trade Convention. The speed with which Baccarat achieved
excellence in this art is astonishing; their millefiori work is shown below
and their pansy weight is particularly famous. The colours they used were
different from other French paperweight makers, being mainly primary.
Baccarat were most active during the period 1845–60. Their antique
weights are never identified on the base, nor do they come in editions.

◀ Pansy Type III

The pansy paperweight
shown here is the
most common – a
Baccarat Type III.
It was a very
popular design
so a lot of them
were made. The
overall velvety
look is obtained by
putting opaque white
beneath the purple petal.
Baccarat flower weights are
usually made in clear glass
and have a star-cut base.
They are never signed, but
the little kink in the stem is
a distinguishing mark of the
company. Additionally, some
of the flowers used in such
weights have buds and
millefiori garlands. These
elements all add to the
desirability of the weights.

Pansy Type III,
1845–60, diam.
7cm/2¾in,
£800–850/
$1,275–1,350

▼ Scrambled weight

Baccarat made very neat
scrambleds. The lengths of
cane are arranged loosely at
right angles to each other;
there are sometimes one or
two cross sections of cane
included as well. The canes
are patriotically coloured in
red, white and blue, with only
the occasional appearance of
another colour, such as yellow.
Baccarat make their canes to
twist downwards to the right
if laid flat. A trick to
remember this is
to think of the
"r" (for right)
in Baccarat.

Scrambled
weight,
1845–60,
diam.
7.5cm/3in,
£350–400/
$550–650

Baccarat canes
Cog canes: Baccarat have
6, 8 and 12 cog canes,
and are the only maker
to use 20 and 22 cogs.

Other canes:

▼ Spaced millefiori weight

This paperweight is a classic Baccarat pattern. The canes rest on "tossed muslin" (lengths of opaque twist) and include silhouette canes. There is a "B1848" cane in this weight, which is actually made up of five separate canes joined together. The most common date is 1848, closely followed by 1847; 1846 is uncommon and 1849 very rare. There are occasionally lengths of coloured canes within the white latticinio but some collectors prefer the latticinio ground to be pure white, with no colour twists.

Spaced millefiori weight, 1848, diam. 7cm/2¾in, **£2,000–2,300/ $3,200–3,675**

Close-pack mushroom weight, 1845–60, diam. 7cm/2¾in, **£1,750–2,100/$2,800–3,350**

▲ Mushroom weight

This paperweight is called a mushroom because of its profile. The mushroom head can be made up of close-pack or concentric canes. Concentric ones are rarer and therefore more expensive. The opaque twist tube with its outer colour twist, known as a "torsade", can occur in blue or salmon. The salmon is the less common and therefore the most expensive. The close-pack head of the mushroom is used in other weights; these are often dated, include silhouettes and cost more than mushroom weights.

Arrow & star   Whorl

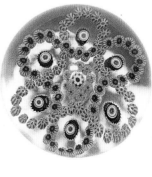

Honeycomb   Fortress

▼ Interlaced trefoil weights

Interlaced trefoil is a common original Baccarat pattern (see below left). Similar weights were produced in the 1930s (see below right) by a maker called Dupont, working at the Baccarat factory. Dupont also made a mustard-coloured pansy weight. His work is not as good as Baccarat's originals as the canework is poor quality and the colours are weak.

Interlaced trefoil, c.1930, 6.5cm/2½in, **£150–250/$250–400**

Interlaced trefoil, with millefiori circlets, 1845–60, diam. 7.5cm/ 3in, **£700–850/$1,125–1,350**

Antique St Louis & Pantin

St Louis has a long pedigree as it was established in 1767 in Lorraine. The firm was granted the right to use the name of Verrerie Royal de St Louis by King Louis XV, who wished to integrate Lorraine into France, having just annexed it. Two lawyers decided to follow Baccarat's lead and established a glassworks in this suitable area. St Louis glass, like Baccarat and unlike Clichy, is made of lead crystal and, like both companies, most of St Louis' antique paperweights have slightly concave bases. (This is a useful tip to use when deciding whether or not a weight is antique.) Pantin were active in paperweight-making about 1880 but their glassworks was established in 1850 under the name of Monot & Company. The name varied until about 1900, when it became fixed as Cristallerie de Pantin.

Scrambled weight by St Louis, 1845–60, diam. 6.5cm/2½in, **£700–850/$1,125–1,350**

▶ **Scrambled weight by St Louis**
St Louis' scrambled weights are popular perhaps because they are bright and relatively inexpensive. When they include sihouette canes, as this one does, the value is increased (one with no silhouettes would fetch around £400/$650). You can recognise a St Louis weight by counting the number of cog canes (multiples of seven are the most characteristic and weights with silhouettes usually have 28 cogs). Also check that the lengths of latticinio twist round to the left – remember "l" for left from St Louis (see Fact File).

▼ **Fruit weight by St Louis**
St Louis is the main maker of fruit weights, although Pantin also made small fruit weights. The fruits usually used are apples, pears and cherries. The cherries also appear in a multi-faceted weight that multiplies the cherries so that they appear to be in a big bunch. There is also a St Louis strawberry weight, a ripe fruit, a ripening fruit and a faceted grape weight (which is rather rare). St Louis made vegetable weights too, but these have a somewhat limited appeal to collectors.

Fruit weight, 1845–60, diam. 5.75cm/2¼in, **£750–950/ $1,200–1,520**

Crown weight, 1845–60,
diam. 6.5cm/2½in,
**£1,500–1,800/
$2,400–2,875**

▲ Crown weight
by St Louis
This is a St Louis classic. In a good crown the stripes should be evenly twisted. The ribbons have a different colour on each side of an opaque white strip. The usual combinations of colours are red and green, blue and red, or blue and yellow, and some aventurine may be added. As with other weights, a diameter of 7.5cm/3in and above is better. The colours and perfection of the central cane are the most important considerations with these weights.

Amber flash bouquet
weight,1845–60,
diam. 5.75cm/2⅛in,
£300–450/$475–725

▲ Amber flash bouquet
weight by St Louis
The flat bouquet, made up of three or more "cane" flowers, is the simplest version of the amber flash bouquet weight. It is quite a nice weight to start with as a simple one can be purchased for around £300/ $475. However, this type of weight is more interesting when it includes a garland and these are not difficult to find. Sometimes the base is diamond cut; this one has an amber flash base and is also charmingly faceted, making it a pretty weight. It is rather unusual, too, in being a miniature. St Louis also made an upright bouquet, which may be garlanded and faceted; this type is expensive.

▼ Fuchsia weight by Pantin
The first documented notes on Pantin weights are dated 1878. Their weights fill the glass and are noticeably larger than the classic makers' similar subjects. Pantin's lampwork appears free-flowing and three-dimensional. Their weights are not dated, and there are no signature canes, so it is always exciting to be able to identify a Pantin.

Fuchsia weight by Pantin,
c.1880, diam. 7cm/2¾in,
£6,500–8,000/$10,400–12,800

Clichy

Clichy was the third of the great French glass and paperweight-making factories of the mid-19thC and was situated on the outskirts of Paris. It was established slightly later than Baccarat and St Louis but soon became a formidable competitor. Sadly, the factory was taken over by Sèvres in the 1880s. The striking thing about Clichy paperweights is their use of soft colours, which are similar to those favoured by the Sèvres factory: rose pompadour, celeste bleu, violette, lapis bleu and a moss green. Another easily recognizable feature is the Clichy rose. Often there is a little indentation where the colour ground meets the clear glass, and on a muslin ground Clichy used parallel strips of latticinio on the base. Of the three principal French factories, Clichy weights are probably the most popular with today's collector.

▼ **Miniature weight with central white rose**

Clichy miniatures are relatively common, so there is a good chance of finding one at fairs and with dealers. Look very carefully at Clichy colours and canes so that you will recognize their weights when you see them. Many Clichy miniatures are concentrics in clear glass, like the one pictured here. The clear glass allows the "skirts" of the pastry mould canes to show up clearly, and a group of pastry moulds with skirts indicates it's a Clichy. This example is in typical Clichy colours, with the bonus of a central white rose.

Miniature weight with central white rose, 1845–60, diam. 4.75cm/1⅞in, **£300–450/ $475–725**

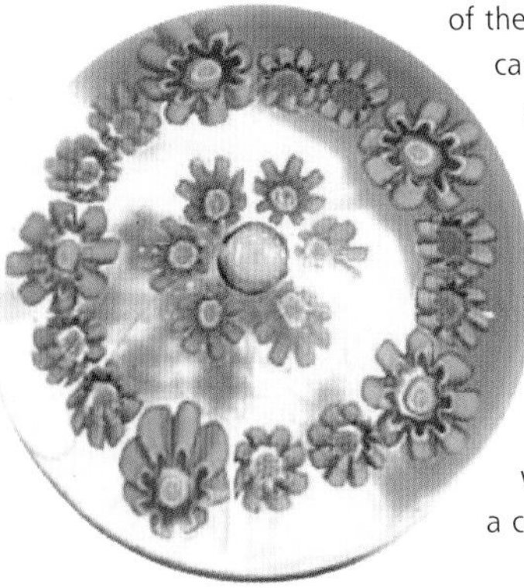

▶ **Two-colour swirl weight**

The swirl is a pattern unique to Clichy. Collectors are always very keen to get one and because of that the price is kept high. Colours vary and three-colour swirls are more desirable than two-colour ones, again adding to the value. But it is the central cane that makes the most difference to the price: if it is a rose cane the price of the weight can quadruple in value. You should expect to pay around £1,000/$1,600 for a two-colour swirl in reasonable condition with a non-rose centre cane, and less for a miniature such as the one pictured here.

Two-colour swirl weight, 1845–60, diam. 5.25cm/2¹⁄₁₆in, **£650–£800/ $1,050–1,275**

"Clichy" is spelt out in turquoise in a circular cane; this occurs in only six known weights, greatly increasing their value.

▼ Pink ground and garland patterned weight

Colour grounds are extremely popular in all paperweights, with or without roses. When there is a rose present then the price is probably doubled. Turquoise is the most common ground colour; violet and apple green are two of the rarer grounds and this pink ground is a little paler than usual. Look out for a white rim around the sides, where the opaque white is showing through, as this indicates that the weight has been repolished.

Pink ground and garland patterned weight, 1845–60, diam. 7.5cm/3in, **£1,400–1,800/$2,250–2,875**

▼ "Barber-pole" weight with pink and white roses

This type of weight is really a development of the basic Clichy chequer weight, which itself is a development of the spaced millefiori on muslin. In the chequer weight, strips of latticinio neatly separate the canes and in the "barber-pole" the latticinio has coloured strands, in this case blue. This is a good example – the colour twists divide it nicely, the latticinio is thick and even, it is a good size and the colours are well balanced. It also has two roses and an unusual "C" in one cane.

"Barber-pole" weight, 1845–60, diam. 5cm/2½in, **£3,500–4,000/$5,600–6,400**

Clichy canes

Below are some examples of common Clichy canes:

Rose   Edelweiss

Six-point star

Pastry mould   Cross

▼ Scrambled weight

A normal Clichy scramble is a bright but softly coloured jumble of canes. It is similar to a roughly made close-pack, but compare the two and you will see the difference. When trying to identify a Clichy, look out for lots of pink and green colours as well as the use of roses, or bits of roses. The commonest colours for a Clichy rose include pink and green and pink and white; more unusual are violet or turquoise.

Scrambled weight, 1845–60, diam. 7.5cm/3in, **£500–600/$800–950**

Old English makers

Old English paperweights remain one of the greatest mysteries in the current world of paperweight collecting. Bacchus paperweights have long been recognizable, but other old English weights have usually been lumped together and called "Stourbridge", for the simple reason that glass has been made at Stourbridge since the 18thC. Recent research has begun to unravel some of the mystery but there still remains a large number of unidentified weights. The idea that Whitefriars made weights in the 19thC has been discredited – it is thought that they, or Walsh-Walsh working for them, put the 1848 date into their paperweights in the 1930s. Because of the recognition problems there are many bargains to be found; look out for quality and buy on that alone. A good weight will have fine, even canes – the central cane must be really central – and have a covering of clear glass.

▼ **Concentric weight by Bacchus**

George Bacchus & Co of Birmingham made large, mainly concentric, millefiori paperweights in the 1850s. They are the only English company to have records of 19thC weights. The example here shows many typical Bacchus canes – you can match them with the Fact File. The question to ask when trying to identify a Bacchus is this: are the canes neatly and uniformly drawn together underneath? If they are not then the weight is not a Bacchus, even if it uses canes that are similar in style.

Concentric weight by Bacchus, c.1850, diam. 8.5cm/3⅓in, **£3,500–4,500/$5,600–7,200**

Unidentified 19thC weight, c.1850, diam. 7.5cm/3in, **£350–450/$560–720**

◀ **Unidentified 19thC weight**

The paperweight shown here is typically English – it is concentric, in clear glass, is 7.5cm/3in, and, if you turn it over, you can see a ring of clear glass on the outer edge and the centre filled up with cane ends that are not drawn together. This is a very fine example, and others can be found of its type. However, there are examples quite different to this one that also have Bacchus-type canes with the same type of base. The highest price for unidentified weights is likely to be around £400–450/$650–725.

Two concentric weights by Arculus, left: dated 1848, but actually c.1920, diam. 7cm/2¾in, **£100–150/ $160– 240**; right: c.1920, diam. 7cm/2¾in, **£100–150/$160–250**

▲ Two concentric weights by Arculus

The two paperweights shown here exhibit the most typical aspects of Arculus weights: the flat profile, pastel shades, slightly uneven concentric pattern and, in some cases, the false date of "1848". If 1848 had been a true cane, it would have at least doubled the price, but, because it is a fake, it makes the undated concentrics as desirable, if not more so, than examples that have a date cane.

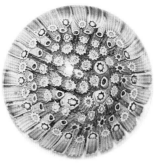

▼ Concentric weight by Richardsons

Richardsons are a famous Stourbridge glass-making firm. The only evidence of their paperweight-making, however, is two dated diagrams, of 1913 and 1914, which are in their archives. These diagrams have made it possible to identify the profiles and paperweight canes used by Richardsons. The weights are usually large, often footed, use a quatrefoil cane and hollow cog cane, and cut their canes precisely so that the base is a reflection of the top.

Concentric weight by Richardsons, c.1913–14, diam. 9.5cm/3¾in, **£350–450/$550–725**

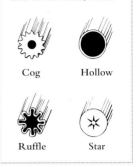

Concentric millefiori bottle by Walsh-Walsh, c.1930, ht 15.25cm/6in, **£350–500/$560–800**

▲ Concentric millefiori bottle by Walsh-Walsh

This firm bought Arculus in 1931 and continued their tradition of making weights. It is not easy to separate the work of the two, but Walsh-Walsh do have a distinctive cane called the "7/6 cane" and their longer outer canes tend to "divide".

"The Last Supper" pinchbeck weight, c.1840 diam. 7.5cm/3in, **£350–500/$550–800**

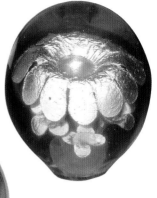

Victorian dump weight, 1850–80, diam. 12.75cm/5in, **£185–205/$300–325**

▲ "The Last Supper" pinchbeck weight

It has not been possible to attribute pinchbecks to any one factory either in England or on the Continent (where they were also made). Most pinchbeck weights were made around 1840 and the material is named after Christopher Pinchbeck (1670–1732), a London watchmaker who invented an alloy that gave the appearance of gold. A large glass lens was placed on top of the stamped pinchbeck picture and then fitted with a base that could be one of several materials, most commonly pewter. Sometimes the pinchbeck is painted, although this is fairly unusual. Other metals or alloys were used as well – silver-effect "pinchbecks" are known, for example. Subjects are biblical, mythological or contemporary to their time.

Dump weight by Kilner, 1829–32, ht 10cm/4in, **£350–400/$560–650**

▲ Dump weight by Kilner

Kilners of Wakefield, Yorkshire, was established in 1829 and in 1832 changed its name to J. Kilner & Son. Sometime before 1844 the "Son" became "Sons". In 1844 it was finally named Kilner Brothers. Kilners stamped their green dumps, although we don't know if they stamped all of them. This example is particularly interesting because it includes other colours in addition to the green. A lot of green dumps were unpopular and ill-used – it is said that they were even used for knocking in nails.

▲ Victorian dump weight

This picture shows one of the many excellent quality Victorian dumps that can be found on the market today. This one has flowers made of silver foil, but many others display delicate flower patterns made by rolling the gather of glass onto a pattern of powdered chalk. It is almost impossible to identify where particular Victorian dumps were manufactured. They were made with the glass that would have been "dumped" at the end of each day by bottle factories making green glass bottles, hence the name. When the bottle-making process became mechanized, the regular making of dumps ceased. However, Hartley Wood & Co, of Sunderland, continued to make Victorian-style dumps until fairly recently.

Varnish glass weights FACT FILE

Edward Varnish and Frederick Hale Thomson made paperweights between 1849–52, using silvered glass. The metal plug in the base (see below) was used to seal the hollow-walled glass and prevent the silver layer inside tarnishing.

Rectangular advertising weight by George J Cockerell & Co, c.1901–20, 10cm x 6.25cm (4in x 2½in), £20–35/$30–55

Print of North Cliff & Sands, Bridlington Quay, 1850–1900, diam. 5cm/2in, £25–35/$40–55

▲ Print of North Cliff & Sands, Bridlington Quay

Once rather scorned, these bits of history are now appreciated by paperweight collectors. The one here is a perfect example: it has human interest, shows the scene clearly and uses bright colours. The older pictures are etchings, the later, 20thC ones, photographs. Examples from the 19thC are round, have curved edges and usually have a dark-coloured, heavy paper backing. Do not put stickers on the back as the paper will come off too.

▲ Rectangular advertising weight by George J Cockerell & Co

This firm obviously decided to advertise that they were coal merchants to the royal family by producing a weight. It must have been made after 1901 because of its "Royal Warrant to the King", who could have been either King Edward VII or King George V. Collectors of these advertising weights, which have now become quite difficult to find, usually like the weights to be engraved in some way.

▼ Circular advertising weight by Northern Assurance Co

Insurance companies must have been very keen on this form of advertising as they are among the most common of examples found. There is little documentation on them and collectors have the fun of sorting out the dates of the companies' existence themselves. As round picture weights are earlier than rectangular ones, the same is likely to be true of advertising weights.

Circular advertising weight by Northern Assurance Co, c.1850–1900, diam. 7.5cm/3in, £25–40/$40–65

Bohemian makers

The term "Bohemian", when applied to paperweights, means that they were made in southern Germany or Czechoslovakia. Bohemian glass of the 19thC is often viewed as the finest glass of that time – in particular, Bohemian cutting techniques were highly developed. However paperweights require different skills from mainstream glassmaking, especially the making of quality millefiori canes and lampwork. A few very fine Bohemian examples of these have survived, but only occasionally do they equal the French examples. This is quite an interesting area of collecting because Bohemian paperweights are not sought after in the way that antique French, English Whitefriars, modern American (Ayotte & Stankard) and Paul Ysart weights are, except in Germany where there is more interest.

▶ **Scattered millefiori weight on tossed muslin ground**
Since the "scattered millefiori" type of paperweight is always associated with Baccarat it is inevitable that this example should be compared with Baccarat too. The greyish muslin has a fair amount of colour twists mixed in with it. The decoration is also quite thin in comparison with a densely packed Baccarat version. The other noticeable difference is the canes – there is much less variety in this Bohemian example than in those of Baccarat, where there is a real richness of colour and shape. However, this weight is still desirable, attractive and interesting – perhaps mainly because of its silhouette canes.

Scattered millefiori weight, c.1850, diam. 7cm/2¾in, **£650–800/ $1,050–1,275**

▼ **Close-pack millefiori weight**
Bohemia covers a large area and historically there were hundreds of glass factories all over the area that is now known as Czechoslovakia. As in any other country, quality varied from one glasshouse to another. The glass is, however, typically rather dark and the canes rest on a spatter base. The canes are usually imperfectly formed, although there may be quite a variety of types. The base is typically flat but rather irregular; some bases have a rough pontil.

Close-pack millefiori weight, c.1920, diam. 5cm/2in, **£40–60/$65–95**

Multi-faceted four-layered flower weight, late 19thC, ht 15.25cm/6in, **£80–120/$125–200**

Amber flash stallion weight, c.1850, diam. 7cm/2¾in, **£250–375/$400–600**

▲ Amber flash stallion weight

The flashed colour on the base of this weight is another typical Bohemian feature of those made in the classic period. Ruby flashing is also quite common. The weights of the type shown here are often faceted, but can also be unfaceted. Animals are a favourite theme. There is also a larger flat series of weights that feature buildings with a caption; these are also usually ruby flashed. Not all amber flashed weights origi-nated in Bohemia – St Louis also used amber-flashing. There is also a deeply engraved variety that has been attributed to Baccarat, but it seems more likely they were made by St Louis. These latter ones are noticeably heavier because they are made with lead crystal.

▲ Multi-faceted four-layered flower weight

Here is another typical Bohemian weight; these are still being made in the area today, which actually makes identification more difficult. Unless you are very familiar with the type your only clue will be wear and tear on the base; the oldest may have some minute chipping along the facets – your eye-glass will be a great help in finding this. For further information on how to distinguish original weights from modern, refer to the listings in the "What to read" section at the back of this book.

▼ Spatter base weight with torchworked name

Spatter base is a recognition point for Bohemian weights generally. Often the torchwork name is in German so that also gives the game away. The Bohemian workers who made this type of weight took their art to the USA and Scotland, so this same style also occurs there too.

Spatter base weight with torchworked name, 1900–30, diam. 7cm/2¾in, **£25–45/$40–70**

Antique American makers

In the middle of the 19thC, when Europe was being riven apart by revolutions, the pull of the New World was considerable. Both English and Bohemian glassworkers went there, so when looking at old American weights it is useful to keep in mind what English and Bohemian weights look like. However, in the New England Glass Company and Boston & Sandwich weights the influence of France is stronger. Below you see the works of those companies, but there were others: the Mount Washington Glass Works was one of the first; Millville were famous for making a rose paperweight on a pedestal; and there was also Dorflinger Glass Works, Pairpoint, Port Elizabeth and the Cape Cod Glass Co. All these companies were working on the east coast of the United States – it was another century before the west coast came into its own.

▼ **Victoria concentric weight by Gillinder**
William Gillinder was born in England and worked in the glasshouses of Birmingham. It is not surprising then that the millefiori weights of Gillinder & Sons of Philadelphia closely resemble those of George Bacchus, Birmingham. Here is an identification tip: Bacchus canes are pulled together underneath, as are Gillinder ones, but Bacchus often show a gap in the middle through which you can see the inside of the weight. Gillinder canes also appear flatter on their base.

Victoria concentric weight by Gillinder, c.1860, diam. 7.5cm/3in, **£600–700/ $950–1,125**

▶ **Poinsettia weight by Boston & Sandwich**
The poinsettia is well suited for use in paperweight designs because of its immediately recognizable shape. Here, the artist has decided to use a purely imaginary blue poinsettia and it is effective against the blue "jasper" ground. The jasper grounds are made of ground-up coloured glass. St Louis also used jasper grounds – it is useful to note that their examples have two layers.

Poinsettia weight by Boston & Sandwich, 1850–90, diam. 6.5cm/2⅝in, **£450–650/ $725–1,050**

FACT FILE

Most common weights
- NEGC and Sandwich poinsettias in red or blue on jasper ground.
- NEGC scrambleds with a reversed date: it looks like 1825, but should be 1852.
- NEGC fruit assortment on latticinio.
- NEGC leaf spray on latticinio.

▼ Kossuth, Governor of Hungary by Boston & Sandwich

The back of this weight is inscribed "Ex-Governor of Hungaria set at liberty by the people of the United States of America". The base is ground and slightly concave, in the manner of classic French weights. Lajos Kossuth was a liberal political leader who fled Hungary to tour Britain and America to drum up support. He was unsuccessful, but must have found favour with the Boston & Sandwich makers. This sulphide was produced at the height of the classic period of paperweight-making, but generally sulphides pre-date millefiori and lampwork weights.

Kossuth, Governor of Hungary by Boston & Sandwich, 1851, diam. 6.25cm/2⅛in, **£200–250/ $325–400**

▼ Assorted fruit weight by the New England Glass Co.

The swirling latticinio ground nicely sets off the arrangement of fruit – this weight was executed by a neat-minded artist who liked symmetry. This is a point of difference between St Louis fruit arrangements and NEGC ones such as this, as St Louis rarely arrange their fruit evenly. Both make their fruit small and central, unlike Pantin whose fruit weights fill the glass.

Assorted fruit weight by the New England Glass Co, 1850–80, diam. 7cm/2¾in, **£250–300/$400–480**

▼ Pear weight by the New England Glass Co.

NEGC did exceptionally well with this design. The fruit, which was about the size of a real fruit, was blown and the base then made separately. The bases were supposed to represent cookies and were fused to the fruit on top. The idea of a fused fruit design was first used by St Louis and Murano. The fusing of the fruit to the cookie base is done at an angle, blossom up and stem down. The blossom is just a blob of dark glass. The surface of the fruit is remarkably lifelike: it was done by streaking the surface with coloured glass, leaving it at different thicknesses to create the shading.

Pear weight by the New England Glass Co,1850–80, diam. 10.5cm/4⅛in, **£750–850/ $1,200–1,350**

Paul Ysart

Paul Ysart moved from Spain to Scotland with his family in 1914 when he was 10 years old. His father, Salvador, was a skilled glassmaker who was given work at Moncrieffs. Here he took on each of his sons as apprentices, starting with the oldest, Paul. During the 1930s Paul Ysart developed an interest in paperweight-making. He and his father made many weights during this period and they sold well, but they were principally employed to make Monart Art Glass (the name "Monart" derived from the "Mon" of Moncrieffs and the "art" of Ysart). Paul Ysart continued at Moncrieffs after World War II and the paperweights from that time originally had a Monart label. Pre-war weights were made with a dark tinted glass; post-war ones had clearer glass. In 1963 he became Training Officer at Caithness. His last move to Harland is described opposite.

▼ **Concentric millefiori weight**
The glass of this paperweight is amethyst-tinted. It is a large weight, as many of the early ones were. It is flat-polished underneath, which is unusual for a 1930s weight. The "PY" (which stands for Paul Ysart) is hidden among the closely packed canes. The makers of millefiori weights have aided collectors by using particular types and colours of canes. When you find an example like this, look out for an eight-pointed "star" with round edges. This may have other canes inside or vice versa.

Concentric millefiori weight, 1930s, diam. 7.5cm/3in, £550–650/ $875–1,050

Sulphide of a horse, 1930s, diam. 7.5cm/3in, £850–1,000/ $1,350–1,600

◄ **Sulphide of a horse**
Paul Ysart made very few sulphides in his career, but when he did he used little cameo brooches, bought from Woolworths, as moulds. In recent years Paul Ysart weights have increased considerably in value as more and more collectors appreciate their quality. Ysart sadly died in 1992 so with supply now limited, his weights are even more sought after, adding considerably to their value. The high price of the weights pictured on these two pages reflects their rarity.

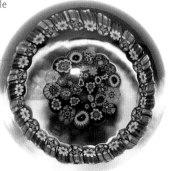

Aventurine flower in a basket, c.1950–60, diam. 7cm/2¾in, **£750–850/ $1,200–1,350**

FACT FILE

Paul Ysart canes

Weights with "H" canes are definitely by Ysart. "PY" canes can be a problem because they were faked. Genuine "Y" canes have the top "v" shape first, then the lower part of the "y" added; dropped "Y"s are fakes.

(H) "H" cane   **(PY)** "PY" cane

Pink "floating" fish weight, c.1975, diam. 7cm/2¾in, **£250–300/$400–475**

▲ Pink "floating" fish weight

This paperweight features an "H" cane. The "H" stands for Harland, the small town in northern Scotland where Paul Ysart set up his own factory in 1971, after leaving Caithness. Ysart made a standard series of weights while at Harland, but they did not all include an "H" cane. Those destined for America had "PY" canes, which was due to the special arrangement he had with American dealer, Paul Jokelson.

Below is a photograph of the "PY" sticker, which is on Harland weights of 1970. Before that date, a rectangular sticker was used.

"PY" STICKER

▲ Aventurine flower in a basket

The basket weight is such a simple, effective conception that when they come up for sale they always fetch a good price. This is a particularly lovely example. The flower is beautifully formed and has a fine aventurine colour. The basket is also delicately made. These weights are not too easy to date as Ysart made them in this size and style throughout his postwar working life. It is always desirable to have a weight with a signature "PY" cane. A few have "P Ysart" on their base; these have provenance as they were sold direct to collectors or given to family and friends.

Rare aventurine snake, c.1963–70, diam. 7cm/2¾in, **£900–1,150/ $1,450–1,850**

▲ Rare aventurine snake

The rounded shape of this weight indicates that it was made at Caithness. Other weights in this important and very desirable type are salamander, fish, three mice and two snakes. Most of these "creatures" have some aventurine on part of their body. The most expensive is the "Two Snakes", at £2,000/ $3,200, as it is very rare.

Paul Ysart ~ 27

Vasart & Strathearn

Paul Ysart was a great paperweight maker, but other members of his family also worked in the glass trade. Salvador, his father, and two of his brothers (the third having died during World War II) left Moncrieff's Glassworks in Perth in 1946 to set up on their own. There had been a difference of opinion in the family and Paul decided to stay at Moncrieff's. The three men, Salvador, Vincent and Augustine Ysart, set up a small glassworks at Shore Road in Perth and called their new firm "Ysart Brothers Glass". During the time they were there, they made art glass similar to Monart glass and called it "Vasart" ("V" for Vincent, "A" for Augustine and "S" for Salvador; the "art" came from their surname). In 1956 Ysart Brothers Glass changed its name to "Vasart Glass". In 1964 it acquired a new building and name when it became Strathearn Glass, with Stuart Drysdale as manager.

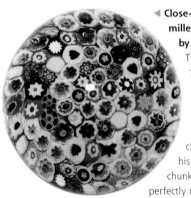

◄ **Close-pack millefiori weight by Salvador Ysart**
The work of Salvador Ysart is very seldom recognized, but it did have certain characteristics: his canes were chunky and not perfectly round in shape. However, the colours he used were, by turns, murky, gaudy (yellow, orange, and purple) or sometimes wishy-washy. He did occasionally put a "Y" cane in his work, but if a weight has a "Y" cane it does not automatically mean it is one of Salvador Ysart's. Other firms use them, including Perthshire who used each letter of the alphabet over consecutive years.

Close-pack millefiori weight by Salvador Ysart, 1930s, diam. 7.5cm/3in, **£125–165/ $200–275**

▼ **Spoke pattern weight by Vasart**
This paperweight is typical of Vasart paperweights. The canes are rather crude and are made in typical Ysart colours, which are continental in nature. A favourite colour combination for this type of weight is orange and purple, with the orange dominating. The best recognition tips are the way the canes stand proud of the ground, that they are not always even and sometimes appear to be in danger of falling over. The pattern of this weight is typical of Vasart too.

Spoke pattern weight by Vasart, 1946–64, diam. 7.5cm/3in, **£45–65/ $70–105**

▼ Close-pack millefiori weight by Strathearn

These are quite common weights. The canes, like those of Vasart, are not perfectly formed, but are of noticeably better quality. Occasionally it is possible to find an example of a close-pack with very finely pulled canes, and that is worth having as Strathearns seldom cost much money and are therefore good value. Normally they are of medium size, about 6.25cm/ 2½in. Close-packs like this, with a colour ground, were most likely made before Stuart Drysdale left Strathearn in 1968 to set up Perthshire (see pp.30–31).

Close-pack millefiori weight by Strathearn, 1964–80, diam. 6.25cm/2½in, **£40–60/$65–95**

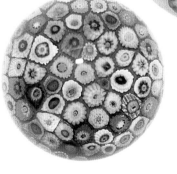

▼ Scattered millefiori weight on tossed muslin by Strathearn

This is a very pretty weight of a type that was later brought to perfection by Perthshire, whose weights illustrate the improvements made by Stuart Drysdale through the years. This weight was also adapted to celebrate the Silver Jubilee. For that it would have had an "ERII" cane and a "77" date cane added. The royal version of this weight could be collectable in the future, although royal commemoratives are quite unfashionable at the moment.

Scattered millefiori weight by Strathearn, 1964–80, diam. 5.75cm/2¼in, **£50–75/$80–125**

Upright flower weight by Strathearn, 1979, ht 10cm/4in, **£50–65/$80–105**

The company history
1946-56: "Ysart Brothers Glass" (Salvador, Vincent and Augustine Ysart)
1956–60: "Vasart Glass" under Vincent Ysart
1960-64: "Vasart Glass" under Stuart Drysdale
1964–8: "Strathearn Glass" under Stuart Drysdale
1968-80: "Strathearn Glass" post Stuart Drysdale
1980: "Stuart-Strathearn" – takeover by Stuart Crystal

FACT FILE

▼ Upright flower weight by Strathearn

Strathearn made a variety of weights, especially after Stuart Drysdale departed with the main makers. This weight was made 11 years after his departure and shows that the remaining makers were not without ideas. They introduced dated weights with signature canes – "S" for Strathearn and a separate "79" cane – and these will always be desirable. They also went into abstracts: for example they produced an attractive "seaweed" weight.

Perthshire

Stuart Drysdale, the Scottish lawyer appointed by Pirelli Glass to manage Vasart, carried on in his managerial capacity when a huge order for glass came in from Teachers Whisky. Teachers themselves went on to build Vasart a new factory, which was called Strathearn. Paperweights continued to be made in the same styles until Drysdale saw a magazine article from the USA about classic French paperweights, which made him realize how far Strathearn still had to go to equal or surpass such beautiful *objets d'art*. He decided then that he only wanted to produce top-quality paperweights, but the owners of Strathearn did not agree with his vision so Drysdale left in 1968, taking the best of the Strathearn workers. With John Deacons, Peter McDougall and Jack Allen, Drysdale created "Perthshire Paperweights" and there he achieved his ambition of making finest quality weights.

▼ **Three-dimensional bouquet weight**
Since 1969 Perthshire have been presenting a new "collection" of around seven weights each year, designated A,B,C,D,E,F and G. Generally they advance in complexity, size and/or quality from A to G. This example was deemed an "F" but in some years it would have been a "G" – it just so happened that in 1990 "G" was an outstanding pedestal weight. Perthshire flowers are a mixture of reality and fantasy. The "P" cane can be seen at the bottom of the bouquet.

Three-dimensional bouquet weight, edition: 300, 1990, diam. 8.25cm/3¼in, **£350–400/$550–650**

Triple overlay weight, edition: 400, 1977, diam. 7cm/2¾in, **£335–450/$535–720**

◀ **Triple overlay weight**
This is a notable weight because, after making the basic weight, it has been overlaid three times and then cut. Each overlaying stage would have risked the condition and saleability of the whole weight. Very few makers have made a triple overlay because of this high risk factor. The edition of this example is 400 (200 for each variation of the flower); one example has pointed petals, the other rounded. Both types are signed with a "P" cane in the centre of the flower.

Penguin weight, edition: 350, 1975, diam. 8.25cm/3¼in, **£350–450/$550–725**

▲ Penguin weight

This is the second design from the hollow-blown series. The inspiration for these weights came from the French classic period, when Baccarat made two hollow-blown weights – ducks in a pond and swans in a pond. Perthshire used these two designs themselves and added another nine. These weights always have a flash overlay. Technically they are different from all others, except that the central figure is lampwork. This is a very collectable series because of the beautiful use that is made of the refractive properties of glass.

DATE CANE

This is an example of a very pretty date cane with the "P" for Perthshire and the date set in one composite cane. Some weights have just a "P" on its own.

▼ Three-colour swirl weight

This weight was "E" in the 1980 series – defining it as a quality weight. Here Stuart Drysdale continued to emulate the classic makers, turning to Clichy for inspiration. You can see here what should always be expected of a Perthshire weight – perfection within the chosen pattern. Perthshire always destroy their "seconds". As with many Perthshire weights, the colours may vary between examples (see the front cover of this book). This is economically sound as Perthshire can use the colours to hand at the time, but it may disappoint collectors who cannot get the colour they first saw in the catalogue. This example is authenticated by a "P1980" cane in the base.

Three-colour swirl weight, edition: 300, 1980, diam. 7.5cm/3in, **£225–300/$350–475**

FACT FILE

Hollow-blown weights
Perthshire's 11 designs:
1973: swans in a pond
1975: penguin
1979: seal
1983: striped ducks
1984: squirrel
1985: polar bear
1987: American bald eagle
1988: kingfisher
1989: frog
1992: giant panda
1998: clown

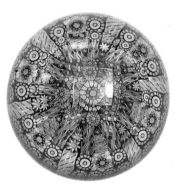

One-of-a-kind millefiori weight, undated, diam. 7.5cm/3in, **£250–300/$400–475**

▲ One-of-a-kind millefiori weight

Perthshire sell their trial weights as one-of-ones (each is unique). With every weight comes a "Craftsman's certificate", to indicate that the weight was not made on the general production lines. These certificates are not dated. The weight pictured has an attractive millefiori pattern; these patterns were issued in limited amounts each year and called "PP" weights, for "Perthshire Paperweight".

Caithness abstract weights

Caithness Glassworks started in the far north of Scotland, in a small town called Wick. The factory came into being in an unusual way: the local laird, Lord Thurso, decided that a glassworks would be an excellent way of bringing work to the sparse local population. The glassworks was to use local sand to make the glass, although in the event this did not work out, and was to be a tourist attraction, which it remains today. The factory prospered and opened two other branches – one in Oban and one in Perth. At present, Caithness' Perth factory is the only one making paperweights, and is, in fact, the biggest paperweight factory in the world. Caithness is particularly famous for its abstract paperweights and it is this style that is illustrated below.

◀ **"Blue Moon" by Colin Terris**

This paperweight illustrates two important points about Caithness. Firstly, they started making abstract paperweights back in 1969 with the idea of four paperweights representing four of the planets. This space theme has continued through the years right up to 1999 when this paperweight was made, which uses laser beams in the production to create an iridescence. The Fact File, on p.33, further discusses the possibilities of this collecting theme. Other makers also use this theme from time to time, such as Selkirk (see pp.36–37).

"Blue Moon" by Colin Terris, edition: 650, 1999, diam. 7.5cm/3in, **£85–95/ $135–150**

▼ **"Fujiyama" by Alastair MacIntosh**

Alastair MacIntosh, like another Caithness designer Helen MacDonald, makes excellent use of the tall type of weight, often slashing off a tongue-shaped front facet. There is a Caithness museum at Perth that displays other weights designed by MacIntosh and MacDonald using the same or other suitable themes. "Alpine Winter", designed by MacIntosh in 1989, is from the mountains theme. Colin Terris' "Sir Percival's Quest" and "Camelot" weights both make good use of the tall shape as well.

"Fujiyama" by Alastair MacIntosh, edition: 650, 1999, diam. 9.5cm/3¾in, **£85–95/ $135–150**

▼ "Sunset" by Colin Terris

In 1980 Colin Terris designed this handsome weight along with three others also featuring solid colour. The production of these was one of the very few times that such a technique was used. The other three weights were "Meteor", "Skyline" and "Winter Moon". At present these weights are very inexpensive. Caithness weights are valuable if there is a lot of cutting involved, as in "Crown Jewel", if the lampwork is very detailed, like "Life's A Beach", if they are an early and popular weight, such as "The Elements Set", or one of a very small edition. Helen MacDonald's weight "Lovebirds" (1995), which combines all of these elements, sold for £795/$1,275.

"Sunset" by Colin Terris, edition: 1000, 1980, diam. 8cm/3⅛in, **£30–50/$50–80**

▼ "El Dorado"

El Dorado is a famous weight among Caithness collectors. Its title refers to the nuggets of gold inside, as envisaged by the seekers of the City of Gold. The front cut-away facet, or lunette, was comparatively new in 1978. The sandblasted back, with its frosted corrugated effect was a little-used idea too. Only 100 were made, and these can vary considerably, so search for a good example.

"El Dorado", edition: 100, 1978, diam. 7.5cm/3in, **£325–450/$520–720**

"Space" theme

Many early Caithness weights follow this theme, the earliest being the Planets Set, now very expensive. Some were inspired by space exploration, others by the stars and planets, such as the delightful "First Quarter", "Star Flower" and "Space Pearl" weights.

▼ Morello paperweight & bottle set

Over the years Caithness have produced beautiful bottle sets, which are now rather difficult to come by. Some bottles, such as the elegant "Enchante" perfume bottle of 1982, were produced singly at very reasonable prices: "Enchante" cost £75/$120. Many were made between 1980 and 1982. If you wish to collect these sets, it is worth putting your name down with a dealer.

Morello paperweight & bottle set, edition: 150, 1999, weight diam. 7.5cm/3in, bottle ht 12cm/4¾in, **£275–325/$450–525**

Caithness other weights

On the previous page were pictured a variety of abstract weights, for which Caithness are famous. They were the originators of such weights and have developed them to their peak. Caithness have, however, also produced many other types of paperweights, a selection of which are illustrated below. Caithness paperweights are not difficult to identify: they have their name and all the details of the weight stamped on the base (the only detail they don't include is the year of issue). Beware of the mark "CIIG", either scratched on the weight, or in a large frosted stamp, as this means Caithness Seconds. Other techniques that the factory have used include overlaying (single, double and quadruple), matt finishing, moulded techniques as backgrounds, exotic and unusual shaping of canes and stencilling techniques.

▼ **Royal wedding moonflower commemorative weight**
The moonflower pattern, with its long inner bubbles, was first made in 1970. This was one of the earliest Caithness weights, and is still in production today. There are many different moonflower variations to collect, including some miniature ones. As a royal commemorative it was issued as a limited edition, unlike most other moonflower weights. In the current market, royal commemoratives are not bestsellers, so there may be bargains to be found.

Royal wedding moonflower commemorative weight, edition: 500, 1981, diam. 7.5cm/3in, **£45–55/$70–90**

Christmas rose sulphide weight, edition: 1,000, 1979, diam. 7.5cm/3in, **£85–125/$125–200**

◀ **Christmas rose sulphide weight**
Caithness have made only a few sulphides. This one is quite subtle: the ground looks black if placed on a surface, but when held up to the light it turns a beautiful blue. The leaves around the rose sulphide are done in a dark aventurine mix that sometimes looks reddish, other times greenish. Since producing this weight, Caithness have continued to experiment with other sulphides but sadly they have not been very successful. Even popular subjects such as the Queen Mother sold only 309 of the intended edition of 1,000, but may one day become valuable.

Daffodils and tulips weight, one of a pair from "Spring Celebration", edition: 50, 1993, diam. 7.5cm/3in, **£275–325/$450–525**

▲ Daffodils and tulips weight, from "Spring Celebration"

"Spring Celebration", originally a set of eight paperweights, was issued in pairs rather than as a complete set. The weight pictured has a pair featuring crocuses. Some collectors look for the the whole set of eight, but these weights stand equally well on their own. They all have the Whitefriars Cane in them, which has been known to cause some confusion because Caithness Glass did not buy Whitefriars Glass. When Whitefriars closed in 1980, Caithness bought their trademark – the White Friar. The weights that followed were in the Whitefriars tradition of classic faceting and neat design, but Caithness used lampwork motifs with a millefiori garland, unlike the simple millefiori of Whitefriars.

▼ Silver dolphin weight commissioned by The Paperweight Shop, York, England

This is a very different weight: it is based on a sphere of glass as many Caithness weights are, but there the similarity stops. The glass is solid black obsidian with a moulded wave effect, and the dolphin is hallmarked solid silver. A similar frog weight was commissioned by the same shop; there were probably only about ten frogs made so they are very rare and hard to find. A magnificent silver lizard was made in a similar style in 1978, in an intended edition of 50, of which only 45 were sold. This very rare lizard weight is now valued at £1,000/$1,600

Silver dolphin weight commissioned by The Paperweight Shop, York, edition: 25, 1986, diam. 7.5cm/ 3in, **£550–650/$875–1,050**

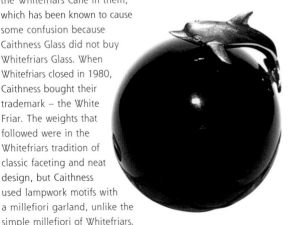

Royal weights

Caithness have made more royal commemoratives than any other paperweight company, covering royal birthdays (the Queen Mother's hundredth will be marked in 2000), royal marriages and other occasions. They can be collected as themes or focusing on one member of the royal family.

Wild orchids weight with lampwork by Allan Scott, edition: 25, 1996, ht 9cm/3½in **£550–600/$875–950**

▲ Wild orchids weight with lampwork by Allan Scott

This delicate piece of lampwork is typical of the maker Allan Scott (see pp.38–39 for his work on "J" Glass weights). This example was heavily cut by Caithness's fine cutter, Martin Murray and displays a lot of exquisite work. Only 25 were made. Most years Caithness make one or two fine weights in small editions. To get one of these you must put your name down early with your dealer.

Peter Holmes & Selkirk

Peter Holmes became involved in paperweight-making through a chance meeting with fellow Scot, Paul Ysart (*see* pp.26–27). Ysart recommended Caithness as a good career move for Holmes from the blacksmiths where he was working part-time. Holmes took up the idea and became an apprentice glassmaker at Caithness. The two men worked together from 1963 until 1970 when Ysart left Caithness to set up on his own. In 1977 Holmes left too, to start up his own firm, Selkirk. Another Caithness employee, Ron Hutchinson, went with him as a business partner. Hutchinson had been Sales Manager at Caithness and so it was a practical partnership, one partner dealing with the creative paperweight-making and the other with business matters. Today, Selkirk has a large visitor centre as well as a glassworks, where large crowds arrive daily to watch the paperweight makers at work.

▼ **Millennium crown weight**
This is an excellent example of a weight made to mark the millennium event. The millennium cane is set in the centre of the top of the crown showing the figure 2000 and the initials "PH" for Peter Holmes. For collectors of crown weights, this one is a must. Holmes made a similar crown weight in 1999, but with no latticinio between the colour twists, and another for the royal wedding of Charles and Diana in 1981 with an identifying cane in the centre. A third crown, dated 1979, has an alternating pattern of twists and latticinio.

Millennium crown weight, edition: 200, year 2000, diam. 7.5cm/3in, **£85–100/$135–160**

▶ **Great crested grebe weight from the "Pond Life" series**
The other three in this series are an otter, trout and frog and water lily; all are copperwheel engraved to the highest standard by David Gulland. Since the quality of this work is superb and the edition is extremely small, this is a very collectable set. Selkirk does not produce many quality engraved or lampwork pieces and when they do the edition is often small. There are a few one-of-ones (only one made) to be found, and since Selkirk lampwork is uncommon these are worth having, as are all quality one-of-one weights.

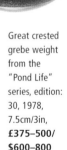

Great crested grebe weight from the "Pond Life" series, edition: 30, 1978, 7.5cm/3in, **£375–500/$600–800** (for set of four)

Marbrie weight, edition: 450
(225 blue and 225 pink),
1980–81, diam. 7.25cm/
2⅞in, **£55–85/$90–135**

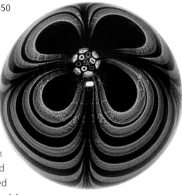

▶ **Marbrie weight**
This weight has a
charming composite
cane in the centre
with colours that
tone together. The term
"Marbrie" is always used
for this kind of feathered
pattern. St Louis (see pp.14–
15) used it in classic times but
it may not have been so successful then as few were made
and they are now very rare and
expensive. Makers do say that
it is a difficult weight to make
and they remain uncommon.
John Deacons (see pp.38–39)
occasionally makes them and
Orient and Flume (see p.54)
make fine, large ones on a
regular basis. Collectors wanting
examples of all types of paperweight should look out for this.

▼ **Mardi Gras weight**
This is just one of a vast range
of very attractive abstract
weights produced over the
years by Selkirk. They are
easy on the eye and will fit
in with any décor as they
come in all colours. For those
who enjoy collecting abstracts,
there are many very pretty
pieces from which to choose.
As Peter Holmes was trained
at Caithness, and was himself
in on the birth of Caithness
abstracts, many Selkirk
abstracts inevitably run
on parallel lines to
Caithness. Some of
their weights with
more complex
patterns come in
limited editions.

Mardi Gras weight,
unlimited, 1998, diam.
7.25cm/2⅞in,
£28–32/$45–50

**Spotting Selkirk
paperweights:**
Make sure it is signed
by Peter Holmes. Selkirk
fully sign all their better
quality weights – with
Peter Holmes name, the
edition details and year.
Look out for the "PH"
cane, illustrated here.

FACT FILE

Sea bed weight, edition: 200,
1979, diam. 7.5cm/3in,
£165–£225/$275–350

▲ **Sea bed weight**
This is an example of Peter
Holmes' imaginative lampwork,
of which he produces a few
each year in small numbers. The
1997 "Twentieth Anniversary
of the Founding of Selkirk"
range included some excellent
examples. One edition, of 20
weights, was presented in a
round wooden box. Others
worth looking out for are the
1980 primroses, the dragonfly,
1979 and the 1980 footed rose.

John Deacons

John Deacons started his career in paperweights at Strathearn in Scotland. When Stuart Drysdale established "Perthshire Paperweights" Deacons went with him, but he left in 1978 and started up his own firm, called "J" Glass. When that folded in 1983, Deacons began again in a simple workshop with no frills, having learnt at "J" Glass that presenting weights in specially made boxes only made them too expensive. Since then his weights have been voted "best value" by the Cambridge Paperweight Circle and 85 per cent of his production is sold to one dealer, leaving him free from the costs of marketing. Be sure only to buy "J" weights from a reputable dealer who can check if they are a known pattern as there are some fakes, often larger in size than the genuine ones. "J" weights, which were limited to just 101 each pattern, are worth more than his later, unlimited Deacons weights.

"J" Glass miniature weight, edition: 101, 1978, diam. 5cm/ 2in, **£90–125/$150–200**

▶ **"J" Glass miniature weight**
Initially "J" Glass specialized in miniatures. Each paperweight measured 5cm/2in (the traditional maximum measurement for a miniature, but this can vary), and each was made in an edition of 101: 100 went on sale and the maker kept one for himself. (John Deacons now owns a wonderful collection of "J" Glass.) After 1978, every weight was dated because of the import laws of the USA that required the date and country of origin. A sticker saying "Made in Scotland" was also added on the base.

▼ **Double overlay weight**
This weight consists of a piece of lampwork, encased in clear glass dipped in colour (often white for the first layer), then dipped again in another colour and finally faceted. This weight is further embellished with fancy cutting around the top layer. The overlay is occasionally encased in clear glass. John Deacons overlays are often sold at £155/$250, which is extremely good value. Expect to pay £300–400/$475– 650) for a double overlay from another maker. The cane in the base, "JD1999" identifies it as a John Deacons paperweight.

Double overlay weight, 1999, diam. 7.5cm/3in, **£155–225/ $250–360**

Identifying John Deacons' weights

FACT FILE

- Amethyst, royal blue and aquamarine transparent grounds.
- Radiating latticinio for flower and butterfly pieces.
- "J" (1978–83), "JD" (from 1983), "JHD" (1995–96) or "StK" (for St Kilda) canes are used.

Crown weight, 1995, diam. 6.25cm/2 ½in, **£65–85/£100–135**

▲ Crown weight

The John Deacons Crown is a classic weight and well worth having. The date cane is in the base. The colours can vary considerably from a simple blue and red to several different coloured twisted ribbons, some of which may have aventurine in them. A few large crowns were made in 1996, but one of the finest versions is a "J" Glass miniature in pink and blue. Other Deacons weights include a large dahlia, patterned millefiori on muslin, marbrie and one-off trial pieces.

Garlanded pansy weight, 1997, diam. 6.25cm/2½in, **£65–80/$100–125**

▲ Garlanded pansy weight

For some years John Deacons has produced all his flower weights with radiating latticinio background and colour coordinated garlands. Before these, his weights had lime-green and white garlands, and at the start they used a whole range of colours. There is no difficulty in recognizing any of Deacon's weights once you handle them, for you only have to turn them over to see the initials and date cane. On 1995 and '96 versions he uses the initials "JHD", for John Henry Deacons. As well as this garlanded pansy, Deacons produces other flower weights with the same background and garlands, such as a clematis duo, a rose and a single pink and white striped clematis.

Large cartwheel weight, 1998, diam. 7cm/2¾in, **£20–35/$30–55**

▲ Large cartwheel weight

There is no date cane or initial to help identify this as a Deacons weight, but in almost every case he includes a neat thistle cane, as here. Other weights made by Deacons that can be found for under £40/$65 are: a medium cartwheel (£15–25/$25–40); a miniature concentric (£10–20/$15–30); a swirl (£30–40/$50–65); one called "Flower in the Rain" (£25–35/$40–55); one known as "Bubbly" (£10–20/$15–30); and two novelty weights, a swan and a teapot (under £20/$30).

DATING CANES

From the first year of production, in 1978, "J" Glass weights sported a "J" cane. When Deacons set up his second company, in 1983, the cane changed to a "JD" motif, as seen here.

William Manson

William Manson started his career as an apprentice at Caithness Paperweights in Wick, Scotland. At the time, the famous Paul Ysart (*see* pp.26–27) was his Training Officer, which gave the gifted young Manson a wonderful chance to learn from one of the best in the trade. When Ysart set up on his own in 1970 he took Manson with him as his apprentice. However, Manson's destiny lay with Caithness because when Ysart's backer withdrew, forcing him to cease business briefly, Manson returned to Caithness on a self-employed basis. He did try to make a go of it on his own at Killwinning in Ayrshire from 1979–81, but, like John Deacons, he found it impossible to carry on and returned to Caithness once again. Then in 1997 Manson decided, with the help of his wife, Joyce, and children, William and Carolyn, to branch out on his own again. This time he was successful, and William Manson Paperweights is still a thriving business today.

▼ **Miniature millefiori weight**

One of Manson's strengths is his ability to make millefiori as well as lampwork. This finely made piece has an aventurine background, but it was considered too dark and the piece never made it to production. This is therefore an extremely rare one-of-one weight, signed by William and Joyce Manson. At 6.25cm/2½in, it would not qualify as a miniature according to old classifications, but several American artists now call their weights miniatures if they measure 6.25–7cm/ 2½–2¾in).

Miniature millefiori weight, 1999, diam. 6.25cm/2½in, **£70–85/ $110–135**

▶ **"Octopus" weight**

In 1978 Manson made his first octopus for Caithness in a series of aventurine creatures including snakes and salamanders, each in a small edition of 50, which have all become very collectable. Manson has continued to make variations on this theme since setting up on his own, some of which are one-of-ones. Such weights might be of an unusual size, or use interesting lampwork on the ground. Snakes and salamanders are traditional lampwork subjects, but Manson is the only one to have made an octopus, making this weight the most highly sought after.

"Octopus" weight, 1999, diam. 9.5cm/3¾in, **£425–500/ $675–800**

▶ Monarch of the Glen

William Manson is a very creative artist who continues to come up with new ideas, such as this, year after year. This is an upright paperweight, a type favoured by Manson. Uprights do not need a stand to be viewed properly. They emphasize the impractical nature of some modern weights, but also have an aesthetic appeal. Along with most quality modern weights, this one is fully signed and dated underneath.

Princess Diana commemorative weight, edition: 10, 1997, diam. 7.5cm/3in, **£300–350/$475–550**

Monarch of the Glen weight, edition: 75, 1999, diam. 7.5cm/3in, **£180–200/$290–325**

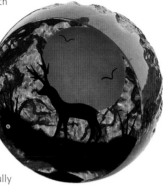

◀ Princess Diana commemorative weight

There were only ten of these weights made, to commemorate the death of Diana, Princess of Wales. They feature the white funeral bouquet that was laid on the coffin by Princes William and Harry. Of all royal memorabilia, those weights pertaining to Princess Diana are likely to be collected most enthusiastically, now and in the future. William Manson has also made a similar series of miniature Diana weights in an edition of 2,000, featuring a pink rose on a blue background. The weight pictured here was available to buy only through Sweetbriar Gallery in Cheshire.

William Manson canes

Throughout his career, whether at Caithness, Kilwinning or in his current business, William Manson has used an identifying "WM" cane in all of his finest, and usually more expensive, paperweights.

▼ Pink dahlia in a basket

For collectors interested in a series of Manson weights, those made at Kilwinning are worth finding. There are two types: the Scotia range (unlimited) and the William Manson Paperweights range (mostly limited to 250). It is not possible to instantly guess which range a weight is from, but the mark on the base of should reveal all – it will either be fully signed with a name and edition number, or have a Scotia label stuck on it.

Pink dahlia in a basket, edition: 150, 1981, diam. 7.5cm/2^7/₈in, **£160–190/$250–300**

Modern English makers

The greatest paperweight-making firm in modern England was Whitefriars. Since their demise in 1980, no one firm has grown large enough to be particularly noticeable, although OKRA do make very fine world-class abstract paperweights. As well as the English firms illustrated below, there are also the following notable firms: Dartington (established by Scandinavians), Merlin (originally named Liskeard), Avon, Thames Valley Glass, Blowzone (once called Osiris), Sunderland Glass, Hand Made Glass Company of Kensington (run by Adam Aaronson), Siddly Langley (mainly surface-decorated), Adrian Sankey, Peter Layton and Patrick Sterne. Minor English makers, such as those featured below, are an interesting collecting field. There is still much research to be done and they can often be found at very reasonable prices.

"Lily Pads" by John Ditchfield at Glasform, c.1980, diam. 8.25cm/3¼in, **£55–60/$90–100**

▶ **"Lily Pads" by John Ditchfield at Glasform**
Ditchfield has been producing art glass since 1973, specializing in iridescent, surface-decorated paperweights as well as lamps, perfume bottles and other related objects. His work is well worth collecting – look for the signature "John Ditchfield, Glasform" on the base (if he did not make it, it will be signed just "Glasform"). Although this weight is listed as "unlimited", about 100 have been made. In big companies, "unlimited" weights are produced in their thousands, but in small firms like Glasform, the maker decides when to stop.

▼ **"Evolution" by Langham Glass**
Paul Miller, the owner of Langham Glass, started as an apprentice with Ronald Stennett-Wilson's Lynn Glass in 1967 and remained there when Wedgwood bought it in 1969. He started up Langham Glass when Wedgwood Glass closed, initially making the abstract paperweights and stylized animals that had been made at Wedgwood. He has recently started making lampwork paperweights. This example is typical of his work from the last two decades. Langham weights are stamped with "Langham" and signed "Paul Miller".

"Evolution" by Langham Glass, edition: 250, 1998, diam 8cm/3¼in, **£80–85/$130–135**

ERII Silver Jubilee by Wedgwood Glass, 1977, diam. 7.5cm/3in, **£50–85/$80–135**

▲ ERII Silver Jubilee by Wedgwood Glass

Wedgwood Glass were a fairly short-lived enterprise (1969–83), but in that time they produced glass that is now much sought after – in particular their glass animals. Wedgwood's fine crystal paperweights are carefully cut, with typical Wedgwood pale blue Jasper plaques showing portraits of royalty and other famous people, and are worth collecting as a series. As well as the example illustrated here, which celebrates Queen Elizabeth II's Silver Jubilee, there are weights of Julius Caesar, William Shakespeare, Charles Dickens and Winston Churchill, among others. All these weights were designed by Ronald Stennett-Wilson.

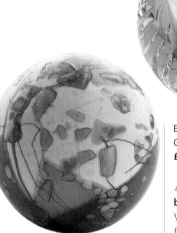

"Larkspur" by Isle of Wight Glass, 1997, diam. 5.75cm/2¼in, **£22–28/$35–45**

▲ "Larkspur" by Isle of Wight Glass

Michael Harris founded Isle of Wight Glass in 1973. Before that he helped establish Mdina Glass in Malta, which is why it is sometimes difficult to match certain patterns with certain factories, since glassmakers tend to carry on using their own successful ideas. Michael Harris was a highly skilled craftsman and those collecting Isle of Wight Glass should look for his signature in particular. After his death a few years ago he was succeeded by his two sons, Jonathan and Tim, who continue to make fine abstract weights.

"Gold Panorama" by OKRA, edition: 1000, 1997, ht 10cm/4in, **£80–100/$125–160**

▲ "Gold Panorama" by OKRA

OKRA started life in a workshop attached to Broadfield House Glass Museum, in Kingswinford. The company progressed, and are now based just outside Wolverhampton, having been bought by Moorcroft Pottery. OKRA weights are not cheap but they are always fine quality objects. The leading designer is Richard Golding and the most highly sought-after weights are those signed by him.

Whitefriars

Whitefriars of London was established as early as 1680 but, sadly for all glass collectors, the factory closed suddenly in 1980. A veil of mystery still hangs over the history of Whitefriars before 1951. It was always thought that the English-style weights with 1848 in bright blue were 19thC Whitefriars weights, but most people now believe these weights were in fact made by Arculus and, later, Walsh-Walsh of Birmingham (*see* pp.18-21). In 1951, Whitefriars started making dated advertising weights and in 1953 dated Coronation weights were made. But it was 1970–80 that was the greatest decade for Whitefriars millefiori paperweight-making. During this time the company produced highly popular weights, and these are the only ones that are known to be absolutely genuine Whitefriars pieces.

▼ **Close-pack, spoke-type pattern weight**
This weight is typical of Whitefriars quality millefiori weights: faceted, fine canes, a regular pattern and green and blue colours. Any Whitefriars fine millefiori weight that has something a bit different in it will cost more to buy than the one shown here. A millefiori weight with red, or pink or yellow in it, for example, will probably be slightly more attractive and collectors may be willing to pay more for this reason. Some of the most beautiful millefiori patterns are those using interlaced trefoils.

Close-pack, spoke-type pattern weight, 1976, diam. 7.5cm/3in, **£225–285/ $350–450**

▶ **Silver Jubilee millefiori crown weight**
Like most china and glass makers, Whitefriars went to town on their Silver Jubilee weights. Records show that 9 different versions were made, including a concentric weight with ribbons and a small crown (edition 1,000), an interlaced trefoil with a small crown (edition 1,000) and a close-pack with a small crown (unlimited). Ink bottles and decanters were also made. The 1978 Silver Jubilee of the Coronation was commemorated with two weights, one a garland with a small orb, the other florettes and a crown.

Silver Jubilee millefiori crown weight, edition: 1,500, 1952–77, diam. 7.5cm/3in, **£225–275/ $350–440**

Advertising weight, 1951,
diam. 7cm/2¾in,
£325–375/$525–600

▲ Advertising weight

This is not a well-made weight and not particularly attractive, but it is rare (if not, it would only be worth £125/$200). An article by David Webber in the Paperweight Collectors Bulletin for 1998 surmises that this was made as a promotional piece for the Festival of Britain in 1951. Only three other Whitefriars advertising weights are known at present, one for the *Illustrated London News*, one for the Gas & Petroleum Industry and one for Windsor Castle.

DATE CANE

The stylized monk in the middle of the cane often looks like no more than a little white comma at first. Between 1972 and 1974 the numbers of the date change from blue on white to white on blue.

Abstract weight, 1970, diam.
7.5cm/3in, **£20–30/$30–50**

▲ Abstract weight

Whitefriars made a range of inexpensive weights, and in fact this was the greater part of their production over the years. The different types include bubble-pattern weights in six colours, all-over cut crystal in clear and amber, various odd-shaped paperweights with clear and coloured glass bubble patterns, swirls in various mixed colours, simple commemoratives with engraved writing or shapes on the base and transfer pictures on a white base. These last are similar to Murano white bases. The shape and weight of the piece should distinguish them: Whitefriars are heavy lead crystal and faceted; Murano are soda glass, unfaceted and wide-based with a low profile.

Faceting Patterns

Whitefriars paperweights are normally faceted. Below are four of the forty-one facet patterns:

Common   Tall dome
window cut   finger cut

Window   Brick cut
& mitre cuts

▼ Christmas weight

These weights (six in the series) are among the most beautiful made by Whitefriars. They are colourful, almost all featuring a light blue base carpet of canes. "The Partridge in the Pear Tree" (1979) uses 9,469 canes and is the most expensive. Other motifs in the series are "Angels" (1975), "Three Wise Men" (1976), "The Nativity" (1977) and "The Christmas Bell" (1980).

Christmas weight, edition: 1,000, 1978, diam. 7.5cm/3in, **£325–375/$525–600**

Modern Baccarat

The modern Baccarat factory remains in the village of Baccarat in north-east France and is still one of the foremost glassmakers in the world, producing quality lead-crystal art glass of all types. In any of the finest gift shops in the world you are likely to find the work of the Baccarat factory. Their production of paperweights is only a fraction of their total glass production, and it is possible that they only continue to make them because of the prestige their weights carry. Like St Louis' paperweights, they continue to be of top quality and expensive and, like St Louis, the Baccarat factory produces a very limited selection of weights for collectors every year. Their weights can only be bought in a very few select shops in each country, but in addition, they do have their own shops in the major cities of London, Paris and New York.

"The Rooster" from the Gridel series, edition: 1,200, 1971, diam. 7.5cm/3in,
£225–300/$350–475

▶ **"The Rooster"**
The present-day makers have picked up this silhouette theme from the antique Baccarat paperweights and made a fine series. The silhouettes were drawn by the young nephew of the Baccarat factory manager and they are still held by the family today. The series comprises 17 images, including a "Squirrel", "Horse", "Elephant", "Pelican", "Swan", "Stork", "Dog" and "Butterfly", made across several years. The cane in "The Rooster" is B1971; one source lists it as 1972 so it probably spans both years.

▼ **Sulphide weight of the Queen and Prince Philip**
As well as being a sulphide, this weight is made especially desirable by being double over-laid in white and a fine glowing red. Made as a small edition, it is highly sought after by all collectors of royal weights. The following year it was made, not as an overlay, in an edition of 1,500 and was almost fully subscribed. The fashion for sulphides, both plain and over-laid, was at its height in the 1970s and Baccarat produced a whole series depicting French, English and Ameri-can statesmen, as did St Louis and Cristal D'Albret.

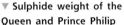

Sulphide weight of Queen and Prince Philip, edition: 195, 1953, diam. 7.5cm/3in,
£200–300/$320–480

Blue butterfly weight, edition: 125, 1978, diam. 9cm/3½in, **£400–550/$650–875**

▶ **Blue butterfly weight**

In the late 1970s and 1980s Baccarat presented one new weight pattern, in various colours, every year, unlike St Louis who have always produced a collection of different patterns each year. This butterfly pattern was made in six colourways. In 1979 four snake weights were produced, in 1980 they made six Dahlias and in 1981 six Frog and Flower weights and four Crocuses. In the 1990s Baccarat produced thematic designs, such as a series called "The Circus" in 1998.

The Gridel Series:
The first of the Gridel weights were made in 1972: "The Rooster and "The Squirrel" (in editions of 1,200). Two were made per year from 1973–75 and then four in 1976. The final two, "The Stork" and "The Red Devil", were made in 1977. After 1972, the editions were reduced to a more realistic 225 or 250.

▼ **Close-pack millefiori weight**
Below is a close-pack millefiori that has canes with symbols of all the zodiac signs. Baccarat also make a much cheaper series of zodiac weights, selling today on the secondary market at about £50/$75; they have a white sulphide zodiac sign on a bright royal blue ground. There is an interesting point to note here: on the base of this weight is an edition number, but no edition limit. Baccarat's fine unlimited weights, such as their series of millefiori patterns on muslin during the 1970s, were also given edition numbers but no set edition limit.

Close-pack millefiori weight, unlimited, 1977, diam. 7.5cm/3in, **£250–350/ $400–550**

▼ **White water lily weight**
This paperweight was made in only one colourway. It is a fine weight as the lampwork is striking and very three-dimensional. It is interesting to note the changes in style that have occurred during the 1990s at Baccarat: the weights are now larger and made in very small editions. For instance, the 1999 "Flower Garden" series of weights were made in editions of 100.

White water lily weight, edition: 250, 1977, diam. 7.5cm/3in, **£350–400/$550–650**

Modern St Louis

St Louis, like Baccarat, were encouraged to make a sulphide paperweight of Queen Elizabeth II for her Coronation in 1953. This they did, but it did not encourage them to start full production of a wide range of paperweights. In fact it was not until the late 1960s that their paperweight production really got going. Both these famous French glassworks are reported to have found great difficulty in rediscovering the lost techniques of their forefathers. St Louis became more interested in paperweight-related objects than Baccarat (something that shows even in the paperweights themselves, which tend to break away from the usual 7.5cm/3in format) and they produced a mixture of paperweight-related items. Below are a collection of weights all made in 1999, to show the great virtuosity in just one year's production.

"La Jardinière",
edition: 100,
1999, diam.
11.5cm/4½in,
**£1,000–1,100/
$1,600–1,750**

▼ **"La Jardinière"**
Vegetables are probably one of the most unlikely subjects to choose for a paperweight, but this rather grand assortment is quite stunning and makes for an unusual and collectable piece. St Louis are one of the few makers to use vegetables: their antique weights included a turnip weight and a radish weight. The sister weight to this one was made by them in 1994 – a pedestal with a fine selection of flowers. The pedestal style of weight is usually used for a magnificent display of concentric millefiori, most memorably done by St Louis for the Chicago Convention of 1973 in an edition of 12, each weight measuring 24cm/9in.

▼ **"Les Demois'Ailes"**
Here we see all the characteristics of a good modern St Louis weight. This is a completely original design and the size is over 7.5cm/3in, which is technically known as a "magnum" weight. It has a very small edition and a high price tag due to its unique style and size. A note worth making about size is that the factories of St Louis, Baccarat, Orient & Flume, Lundberg Studios, Steven Lundberg Art Glass and Rick Ayotte all produce paperweights over 7.5cm/3in as their standard sized weight.

"Les
Demois'Ailes",
edition: 100,
1999, diam.
9cm/3½in,
**£900–1,000/
$1,450–1,600**

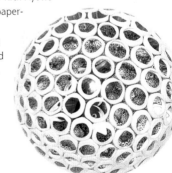

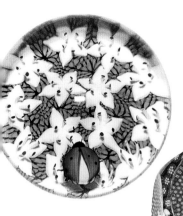

FACT FILE

Collecting St Louis
St Louis paperweights are top of their market and therefore an expensive investment. One way of collecting them is to choose just one a year, or perhaps several of their earlier editions, which are considerably less expensive. You could also choose a theme, such as sulphides or flowers.

"Fleur d'Ange", edition: 150, 1999, diam. 8.5cm/3⅜in, **£825–925/$1,325–1475**

▲ "Fleur d'Ange"
This is another beautifully made paperweight, but when you are spending this amount of money, do compare the weight you are offered with one in a St Louis brochure as the brochure will show you the sort of quality it ideally should be. The weight shown above includes a ladybird, which is not simply a "cute" little addition but is used as the main design feature. William Manson in Scotland and Ken Rosenfeld in the USA also include ladybirds frequently and effectively in their paperweight compositions.

"Envol", edition: 150, 1999, diam. 8.5cm/3⅜in, **£700–800/$1,125–1,275**

▲ "Envol"
Here a millefiori dove sits on a millefiori branch sprouting millefiori leaves, under a beautfiul blue millefiori sky. In 1982, St Louis produced a blue-pattern millefiori butterfly on a white carpet ground. The factory has produced a large number of wonderful millefiori patterned weights, but this one, above, and the 1982 butterfly weight are the only millefiori "scenes" to be created by St Louis.

▼ "Un Vent de Paradis"
St Louis made only 75 of this highly regarded design and it sold out almost immediately. It is a wonderfully original conception: the complete weight is covered in a beautiful selection of brightly coloured canes, and at regular intervals on the side are "portholes" through which you can see the butterfly inside (and the top of the weight is faceted to reveal a full view). Like all St Louis weights, the edition number is acid-etched on the base and the "SL" and date are within a cane.

"Un Vent de Paradis", edition: 75, 1999, diam. 9cm/3½in, **£1,150–1,250/$1,850–2,000**

Modern American makers

The USA is the dynamic centre of the modern paperweight world. It was there that Paul Jokelson, dealer and collector, inaugurated The Paperweight Collectors Association, which began as a purely American club but is now the most influential paperweight organization in the world. In the 1950s and 1960s new paperweight makers were few and far between, being limited to Charles Kaziun and a few others. Today there are a dozen or more top-class makers operating in their own studios, plus several bigger concerns. The pattern of paperweight production is different in the USA to the rest of the world – in the USA there are a number of quality makers working independently whereas in Britain and France there are mainly large glassworks, with smaller makers less important. Individual American makers sign their weights but do not always declare the edition, nor provide a certificate or box.

▼ **Bouquet weight by Paul Stankard**

This is quite an ordinary weight by Paul Stankard's standards and compares with the work of Chris Buzzini (see opposite page), for botanical accuracy. Stankard developed a rather unusual style by including, among the leaves and stems, little people like tailor's dummies and plaques with words such as "fertile" on them. His lampwork is considered the finest, but it is not easy to spot a Stankard at first glance. Look for a signature cane or inscription; he uses a range of colours in his "S" cane, by way of dating his weights.

Bouquet weight by Paul Stankard, 1986, diam. 7.5cm/3in, **£1,550–1,800/$2,475–2,875**

"December Morning" by Rick Ayotte, 1999, edition: 25, diam. 9cm/3¼in, **£650–750/$1,050–1,200**

◀ **"December Morning" by Rick Ayotte**

Rick Ayotte has been making paperweights since 1970 and early on became friends with Paul Stankard. Ayotte's lampwork is astonishing: he can fashion a blueberry with a "bloom" on its surface, but he is best known for his birds. His weights are usually easy to distinguish from Buzzini's and Stankard's because there is a flamboyance about them – full of interest and usually large (although he does make some miniatures). The weights are a distinctive shape too, like a large disc with rounded edges

▼ Bouquet weight by Chris Buzzini

This paperweight is, as usual, more colourful than the Stankard bouquet – one way of distinguishing between them. His signature, "Buzzini 88", is inscribed on the side. Up until 1990 each of his weights were signed with a cane, which included the word Buzzini and the year, but after that date he stopped using the cane. Before branching out on his own in 1986, Buzzini worked with Lundberg Studios, Orient & Flume and Correia Art Glass. His weights have rocketed in price in the last few years, probably because they are so similar to those made by Paul Stankard.

Bouquet weight by Chris Buzzini, 1988, diam. 7.5cm/ 3in, **£750–900/$1,200–1,450**

▼ Raspberries & blossom weight by Randall Grubb

Randall Grubb makes highly realistic weights. This lovely example is made even finer by the unusual addition of trellis cutting on the back. With all such fine modern weights it is important to look for a signature or identifying cane. Weights made by Grubb from 1986–91 will have a signature and date. Post-1991 he has used a black signature cane on white ground.

Raspberries & blossom weight by Randall Grubb, 1995, diam. 8cm/ 3⅛in, **£600–700/$950–1,125**

Buying modern American weights:
Decide on a style that appeals and see the "What to read" and "Where to see" sections at the back of this book for details of publications, dealers and websites. There are probably four times as many excellent dealers and museums in the USA than those listed, so contact the PCA for details.

▼ Orchids with roots by Mayauel Ward

This beautiful paperweight is by Californian artist, Mayauel Ward, who works for Abelmann Art Glass. Ward makes paperweights in his spare time and produces just 50 or so a year. In spite of this, his work ranks among the best. His recent weights are fully inscribed, with no signature cane; before 1995 he used a stylized signature cane of an "M" over a "W", just touching.

Orchids with roots by Mayauel Ward, 1997, diam. 5.75cm/2¼in, **£250– 300/$400–475**

Modern American family firms

Quality paperweight-making has been happening long enough in the United States for a tradition to have grown up in some families. The Lundbergs, Trabuccos, Banfords and Tarsitanos are all into their second generation of makers, although in the case of the Banfords and Tarsitanos, the different generations were in at the start of the business together. The Lundbergs may cause some confusion for collectors now because Steven Lundberg recently left his old family firm to set up his own independent company, Steven Lundberg Art Glass, so there are now two "Lundberg" firms. Many talented American makers choose to make all their paperweights, even the finest and most expensive, "unlimited", which allows them the freedom to produce an unspecified amount. This is true of all the makers featured on this page, hence no edition numbers have been given.

◀ **Dragonfly lagoon weight by Steven Lundberg**

This is one of Steven Lundberg's finest and most inventive paper-weights. It is a design he took with him when he set up on his own, but if you see one of these weights it is more likely to be from his days in Lundberg Studios. This weight has torchwork inside – painting with coloured glass to produce a flowing two-dimensional effect. It is typical of the work of Lundberg and Daniel Salazar, with whom he worked at Lundberg Studios. Lundberg's son, Justin, now works with him at Steven Lundberg Art Glass. The weights are fully inscribed on the base.

Dragonfly lagoon weight by Steven Lundberg, 1996, diam. 8.5cm/3⅜in, **£285–325/ $455–520**

▼ **White crane weight by Daniel Salazar at Lundberg Studios**

This beautiful paperweight comes in the standard size seen here, with a white crane and blue iris, in a miniature size with just a white crane, or a magnum size with two cranes and an iris. Daniel Salazar joined James and Steven Lundberg soon after they set up the Studios, but only Salazar now remains (James Lundberg recently died). Salazar's weights have a torchwork "DS" in the base and are fully inscribed around the edge.

White crane weight by Daniel Salazar at Lundberg Studios, 1995, diam. 8.5cm/3⅜in, **£290–£345/ $475–550**

Snake by Victor Trabucco, 2000, diam. 8.5cm/3⅜in, **£600–700/$950–1,125**

◄ Snake by Victor Trabucco

Victor Trabucco has been making fine paperweights such as this since the 1970s. By the 1980s his twin sons, David and Jon, were also making high-quality paperweights. It is often easy to spot the work of the Trabuccos as their flowers have a satiny look to them. Victor himself makes fine magnums with various flower designs, but he is mainly known for his salamander weight, which was inspired by the Pantin original. This weight, like other Trabucco weights, is signed on the side and has a "VT" cane. His sons use the "T" on its own as their signature cane, and also fully inscribe their weights.

▼ Lily-of-the-valley gingham overlay weight, Bob Banford

Like Victor Trabucco, Rick Ayotte and others, Bob Banford likes to be versatile in his lampwork designs. He and his father, Ray, set up their studio together in the early 1970s. They are both famous for their gingham-cut overlays, sometimes resembling a basket, which makes them more expensive. Bob Banford's wife, Bobbie, made weights too, starting in the mid-1980s and continuing until the late 1990s. Her weights are usually about 7cm/2¾in and are strikingly neat flower arrangements, often with blues and yellows. Bobbie used a turquoise "B" as her signature cane, Ray uses a black "B" in a white cane and Bob a red "B" on a white cane with a blue edge.

Lily-of-the-valley gingham overlay weight by Bob Banford, c.1980, diam. 7.25cm/2⅞in, **£800–900/ $1,275–1,450**

Dahlia bouquet weight by Debbie Tarsitano, 1980s, diam. 8cm/3⅛in, **£700–900/$1,125–1,450**

▲ Dahlia bouquet weight by Debbie Tarsitano

Debbie Tarsitano is a fine lampwork artist. She worked with her father, Delmo (who is most famous for his salamander weight) until his death in 1991, and also with Maz Erlacher, a renowned engraver. Tarsitano's weights are very original and very expensive, fetching up to £1,000/$1,600 according to the amount of detailed engraving.

Modern American other makers

In addition to the individual lampworkers and family firms mentioned on the previous pages, there are a number of other important American paperweight makers. Five are illustrated below, but one of the other most significant names is Charles Kaziun, who started making paperweights in 1939. He made fine lampwork and was known for miniature paperweight-related perfume bottles as well as Millville-type roses. Other highly skilled makers include the Kontas brothers – they make fine orthodox lampwork weights, but mostly for themselves so it is a rare occasion when their weights come on the market. Gordon Smith and Johne Parsley are both top-quality lampworkers, as are the Sikorsky-Todds family, who make torchwork scenes in their paperweights (*see* Fact File p.53). There are other makers too numerous to mention here.

▶ **Asian magnolia weight by Orient & Flume**
This company's rather strange name has a simple explanation: their glassworks are situated at the junction of Orient and Flume Streets in Chico, California. Their work is very similar to that of the Lundbergs, apart from a few minor differences. One of these is that Orient & Flume do produce limited editions of weights. Their style is a little bolder than the Lundbergs', and often their weights are larger than those of their counterparts.

Asian magnolia weight by Orient & Flume, edition: 300, 1999, diam. 7.5cm/3in, **£175–215/ $275–350**

▼ **Perfume bottle by Correia**
This bottle is typical of the early work of Correia because it is iridescent. Many of the company's early weights were based on developing Tiffany-style techniques and they used surface decoration then more than they do now. They have used many different techniques in new and exciting ways, such as in their superb marbrie weights. Correia produce acid-etched weights of cats and dogs, with a black silhouette against a dull background through which shines a central ball of colour, as well as paperweight-related items, like the bottle pictured here. All are signed "Correia" on their base.

Perfume bottle weight by Correia, c.1980, ht 16.5cm/ 6½in, **£55–65/$90–105**

▼ Miniature pumpkin weight by Ken Rosenfeld

Ken Rosenfeld is one of a group of paperweight makers living in Oregon. One of his most famous weights is his "Pumpkin Patch", a standard-sized weight (unlike the miniature one pictured here) featuring three pumpkins and showing gradations of colour in both the fruit and its leaves. It sold fantastically well but was an extremely difficult weight to make and a number of weights had to be thrown away as they were damaged in the process. So the "Pumpkin Patch" had a very limited production run, making it a very desirable weight. However the miniature pumpkin weight, as seen below, is still available.

Miniature pumpkin weight by Ken Rosenfeld, 1997, diam. 6.25cm/2½in, **£160–180/ $250–290**

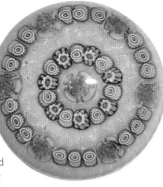

Concentric weight by Parabelle Glass, edition 10, 1998, diam. 7.5cm/3in, **£400–600/$650–950**

▲ Concentric weight by Parabelle Glass

Parabelle is the trade name of Doris and Barry Scrutton of Oregon. They are quite unusual artists as they make their own colours and also make mille-fiori weights. Most US makers work in lampwork rather than millefiori, although one other maker, Drew Ebelhare, makes fine millefiori that is reminis-cent of the French classics. (Ebelhare's weights are identified by a yellow "E" cane or a signature on the base). Parabelle weights are usually 7.5cm/3in and use very distinctive canes – mainly an original pansy cane and their variety of the Clichy rose. The small editions make their weights particularly desirable. Parabelle weights have a very neat signature cane, PB1998.

Paperweight-related items

Items with millefiori or lampwork, or connected to paperweights in any way, make an interesting collection theme. The many different items include wafer trays, shot vases, candlesticks, newel posts, door knobs, scent bottles, plaques, tumblers and millefiori jewellery.

▼ "Spirit" by Ed Nesteruk

Ed Nesteruk has an engineering background and is an expert on glass colours. He usually uses a tall format and silver-veiled designs of supreme quality. He sticks to different shades of pastel colours and uses a high lead content crystal to give his paperweights sparkle and substance. All Nesteruk's weights are signed and dated. Similar weights were made by Michael O'Keefe, up until 1990.

"Spirit" by Ed Nesteruk, 1999, ht 12cm/7½in, **£140–160/$225–250**

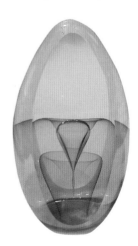

Chinese & Indian makers

Paperweights have been exported from China since the 1930s, when an American businessman asked Chinese glassmakers to copy antique French weights. They were not very successful and there is little danger of Chinese weights being mistaken for French. The oldest Chinese weights have tinted, often yellowish, glass and a strange, soapy feel; more recent weights are in clear glass. Most Chinese weights have irregular, frosted bases, but frosting does not guarantee a Chinese origin as some 1930s Bohemian weights also have frosted bases. Colour is another identifying factor – yellow and orange canes are particularly popular with Chinese makers. There are only three Indian patterns: the three-flower spatter pattern is by far the most common. It is not known for certain in which area or city Chinese or Indian weights were made, but the name "Shantung" Glass is often on the boxes of Chinese weights.

▼ **Indian three-flower spatter pattern weight**
These weights do sometimes have "Made in India" labels on them, which makes them easy to identify, but this flower pattern is India's most common choice, and therefore easy to spot anyway. To call it three-flowered is perhaps misleading, because the "flower" is simply a spatter of coloured glass, shaped with a stem and burgeoning round a splash of colour.
The Bohemians were fond of the spatter pattern too, but it mainly appeared in the bases of their weights. Indian bases, like Chinese, are frosted.

Indian three-flower spatter pattern weight, c. 1930, diam. 5cm/2in, **£3–6/$5–10**

▶ **Chinese three-flowered bouquet weight on latticinio**
This is a typical example of a Chinese copy of a French weight. The three flowers and the latticinio are there, but there is little else to compare with the original French weight. These weights are soapy to the touch and have a flat base with no sharp edges, quite unlike the neat, slightly concave base of the French weights. The base of this weight, above, is also showing wear. The Chinese pansy weight is the best of the copies, and actually much rarer than the French version.

Chinese three-flowered bouquet weight on latticinio, 1930s, diam. 5cm/2in, **£15–30/$25–50**

Chinese white ground weight with painted panda, c.1930, diam. 7cm/2¾in, **£45–60/$70–95**

▲ Chinese white ground weight with painted panda

This type of weight is quite beautiful and cheap to buy, but unfortunately difficult to find. There are at least two different versions of the painted panda weight. The Fact File, right, talks further about white grounds, which can have other subjects such as birds, cats and squirrels. The miniature versions are particularly attractive and the landscapes are delicately painted. These Chinese weights are particularly popular with dealers.

▼ Chinese millefiori weight with two primitive bird silhouettes

This is an interesting weight, from a factory that often marked its weights with a red rose, although the rose is not visible on this weight. Sometimes it is hard to make out the bird silhouettes (probably intended to be pigeons) but they are always in red, white or blue. This same factory makes stylized tree weights in two shades of green. Sadly, no information exists as to where the company was based.

Chinese millefiori weight with two primitive bird silhouettes, post-World War II, diam. 5cm/2in, **£20–30/$30–50**

Chinese flower weight, post-World War II, diam. 9cm/3½in, **£25–35/ $40–55**

▲ Chinese flower weight

These flower weights are very good value –they can be found for less than the price quoted here but are often mistaken for being worth a lot more. The centre of the weight has yellow stamens and nicely shaded petals. Recently, the Chinese makers have also produced excellent fish weights and salamanders, which, like these flowers, provide excellent value for money with prices ranging from £15–50/$25–80.

Other paperweight makers

Collecting paperweights is now a huge international market. Collectors worldwide can buy through the Internet or through advertisements in paperweight literature from dealers in the USA and Europe. It is likely, therefore, that information on paperweight makers around the world is now reasonably complete, especially with the explosion of the Internet and the ease with which different countries can communicate. Featured below are a few makers who have not fallen easily into one of the categories or countries already covered in this book, but who play an important part in the paperweight-making world. However, the range of makers does not end here, as there must be many independent artists around the world who sell well within their own country, but who have not yet come to the notice of collectors on a global scale.

Val St Lambert weight, Belgium, c.1880, 8.5 x 6cm/3⅓ x 2⅓in, **£250–300/$400–475**

▶ **Val St Lambert weight, Belgium**
This paperweight has a very classic 19thC look about it – it was produced at a time when Bohemian glass was regularly made in a flashed ruby colour and both English and Bohemian glass were heavily cut. Val St Lambert was founded in 1825 in Belgium and the company's wide variety of weights include spaced millefiori, patterned millefiori, concentrics, muslin grounds and colour grounds, flowers, sulphides and overlays. Their faceting is always very concave and their bases are flat.

▼ **John & Jackie Kennedy weight, Cristal d'Albret, France**
Cristal d'Albret is a glassworks in Vianne, France, that has been making sulphides since 1966. Like other sulphide makers, during the 1960s and 1970s Cristal d'Albret chose famous world figures, chiefly American, as their subjects. Their most valuable sulphides are the two Churchill weights. The overlaid version of this Kennedy weight is probably the second most valuable. The price given is based on both the edition number and the subject's popularity.

John & Jackie Kennedy weight by Cristal d'Albret, France, edition 2,000, 1967, diam. 7cm/ 2¾in, **£85–100/$135–160**

Collecting off the beaten track:

Collecting largely unknown makers is exciting but not without its risks, and may require some travelling. It is best to decide first what type of weight is of interest and the maximum price you are willing to pay. Much of Eastern Europe, Asia, Australia and Africa remain unexplored as yet.

▼ **"Monet's Garden Series, Spring" by Peter Raos, New Zealand**

Peter Raos' paperweights are marketed mainly in the USA. "Spring" seems to be the most popular one of the "Monet's Garden Seasons" series, but there is also "Spring Perfume". The "Spring", "Summer" and "Winter" weights are quite similar in colour and design, but the "Autumn" one, known as "Madame Butterfly", has an amethyst background with small white flowers. Raos also has a series called "Georgia O'Keefe", with three Calla-type lilies in the style of O'Keefe paintings, and he is developing a "Rock Pool" series using traditional lampwork techniques.

"Monet's Garden Series, Spring" by Peter Raos, New Zealand, 1997, ht 8.25cm/3¼in, **£90–115/$145–185**

▼ **Orrefors weight, Sweden**

So few Swedish weights appear on the English market that very few collectors are looking for them. Those that do surface are probably bought by collectors of Scandinavian glass generally, or else are just bought casually because they are attractive, a little different and usually not very expensive. They are good quality, normally abstract, often geometric in shape and most commonly clear glass (but this one is unusual in that respect). Orrefors, Kosta Boda and Studio Ahus are well-respected names.

Orrefors weight, Sweden, c.1960s–70s, ht 10cm/4in, **£40–60/$65–95**

▼ **Mdina weight, Malta**

Mdina weights are produced on a prolific scale and are found at most antiques and collectables fairs in Britain. The colours are nearly always swirling blues and greens, thought to represent the Mediterranean Sea. The artist Michael Harris worked for the Mdina factory (see pp.43). Some weights are signed "Mdina", others are not. Two other Maltese paperweight factories are Gozo Glass, on the island of Gozo, and Phoenician Glass, both of which make surface-decorated weights.

Mdina weight, Malta, post-1950, ht 7.5cm/ 3in, **£20–30/ $30–50**

Glossary

Annealing Cooling slowly so the paperweight does not crack

Aventurine Usually a gold colour, but can be red or green or blue according to what metallic particles are added to the mixture; also known as goldstone

Baseplate The heated metal surface onto which the lamp-work is placed and kept warm

Basket Latticinio radiating out from the centre of the base of a paperweight and stopping half-way up the side of the paperweight to form a "basket" holding the motif

Cane A cross-section of a stretched rod of glass

Carpet ground Repeated canes forming a "carpet" over the base of the paperweight

Chequer A paperweight pattern made to resemble a chequer-board; large canes separated by strips of latticinio

Classic Period 1845–60

Clear ground The paperweight motif is set in clear glass

Close-pack millefiori The canes are set tightly together

Cog cane A cane with a serrated edge

Concentric The centre of the weight is a single cane encircled by larger circles of canes

Crown paperweight Starting from a centre point at the top of the weight, which may have a central cane, latticinio and coloured ribbons radiate out

Crowsfoot Another term for an arrow cane

Cushion A term meaning the ground of the paperweight

Double overlay The weight is dipped in two different colours (overlays) and is then cut

Dump A piece of green bottle glass used to make a doorstop, paperweight or ornament

Encased overlay A double overlay encased in clear glass

End-of-day Another name for scrambled, or macedoine: left-over pieces of cane mixed together without a pattern (although Baccarat scrambleds do have some sort of pattern)

Facets Cuts, normally concave, through which the central motif of a paperweight can be seen

Filigree Twisted opaque white canes or twisted coloured canes; some authorities use the word filigree for coloured twists and latticinio for white twists

Flash A thin layer of transparent colour

Flat bouquet or nosegay A two-dimensional bouquet placed parallel with the base of a paperweight

Floret (florette) A large complex cane, resembling a stylistic flower head

Flute A thin finger-like groove used as decorative cutting in some paperweights, particularly Whitefriars

Garland A chain of canes forming a circle or more

complex pattern, usually around a central motif

Gather This is the large blob of glass that adheres to the pontil rod when it is put in the furnace.

Hollow blown A paperweight with a central cavity

Jasper Ground coloured glass mixed to form a background

Lace Strips of latticinio, also known as muslin or tossed muslin, which form a ground

Latticinio Lengths of white opaque twist glass, sometimes called filigree, muslin or lace

Magnum A weight of over 7.5cm/3in in diameter (some say 10cm/4in because of the larger size of American weights)

Marbrie A paperweight decorated with feathering, usually coloured loops on white

Marver A flat metal surface on which the gather of glass on the pontil rod is shaped by rolling it backwards and forwards

Metal The technical term for molten glass

Millefiori Italian word meaning "a thousand flowers", also meaning a group of canes

Miniature A paperweight under 5cm/2in

Pastry mould A cane which has been pressed down to form a skirt around itself; a technique particularly used by Clichy

Pinchbeck An alloy of copper and zinc

Pontil mark The mark left when the paperweight is

knocked off the pontil rod. This mark is usually polished off.
Pontil rod The iron rod used for gathering glass and subsequently fashioning it at the glassmaker's chair
Rosette Cluster of canes
Scattered millefiori Millefiori patterns, particularly on muslin; usually the canes are spaced rather than scattered, but either term can be used

Star-cut A star cut into the base of a paperweight, particularly used by Baccarat
Sulphide Another word for a cameo in a paperweight
Template A cast-iron patterned plate into which millefiori is fixed
Torsade A latticinio and filigree twist encircling a paperweight motif, particularly mushrooms
Upright bouquet A bouquet made up of cane flowers or

lampwork flowers, standing upright in the paperweight as opposed to a flat bouquet, which lies level with the base of the paperweight
Upset muslin Strips of latticinio used as a ground
Window A cut, or slice, off a paperweight through which one can view the motif inside; also another word for a facet

What to read

GENERAL REFERENCE BOOKS
Bergstrom Mahler Museum, New York *Glass Paperweights* (United States Historical Society Press, USA, 1989)

Dohan, Andrew H. *Dictionary of Paperweight Signature Canes* (Paperweight Press, USA, 1997)

Flemming & Pommerencke *Paperweights of the World* (Schiffer, USA, 1993)

Hollister, Paul *Encyclopaedia of Glass Paperweights* (Clarkson N Potter Inc, USA, 1969)

Jargstorf, Sybille *Paperweights* (Schiffer, USA, 1991)

Reilly, Pat *Paperweights* (The Apple Press, London, 1984)

Selman, L.H. *All About Paperweights* (Paperweight Press, USA, 1985)

Selman, L.H. *Art of the Paperweight* (Paperweight Press, USA, 1988)

SPECIALIST PAPERWEIGHT BOOKS
Ayotte, Rick *Songs Without Words, The Art of the Paperweight* (Paperweight Press, USA, 1997)

Hall, Robert *Old English Paperweights* (Schiffer, USA, 1998)

Hall, Robert *Scottish Paperweights* (Schiffer, USA, 1999)

Hawley, John D *The Boston & Sandwich and New England Glass Companies* (Paperweight Press, USA, 1997)

Ingold, Gerald *The Art of the Paperweight – St Louis* (Paperweight Press, USA, 1995)

Jokelson, Paul *Sulphides, The Art of Cameo Incrustation* (Thomas Nelson & Sons, USA, 1968)

Kulles, George N. *Identifying Antique Paperweights – Millefiori* (Paperweight Press, USA, 1985)

Kulles, George N. *Identifying Antique Paperweights – Lampwork* (Paperweight Press, USA, 1987)

Mahoney & McClanahan *The Complete Guide to Perthshire Paperweights* (Paperweight Press, USA, 1997)

Stankard, Paul J. *Homage to Nature* (Harry N Abrams Inc, USA, 1996)

Terris, Colin *Caithness Paperweights* (The Charlton Press, USA, 1999)

Turner, Clarke & Andrews *Ysart Glass* (Volo Edition, London, 1990)

Where to buy and see

Quality auction houses worldwide sell paperweights as part of their glass sales; the New York branches of Christie's and Sotheby's may also have dedicated sales. Additionally, auctions are held on the Internet. If buying from a dealer, ensure that they are PCA (Paperweights Collectors Association, Inc.) accredited; contact the PCA for details. Before visiting any museums, speak to the curator of the glass department as weights may be in store or out on loan.

MAJOR AUCTION HOUSES

Christie's King Street
8 King Street, St James'
London SW1Y 6QT, UK
Tel: 020 7839 9060

Christie's New York
Rockefeller Centre
20 Rockefeller Plaza
New York, NY 10020, USA
Tel: 001 212 636 2000

Sotheby's
34–5 New Bond Street
London W1A 2AA, UK
Tel: 020 7293 5000

Sotheby's New York
1334 York Avenue
New York, NY 10021, USA
Tel: 001 212 606 7000

SPECIALIST DEALERS
Farfalla-Paperweights
Peter Pommerencke &
Monica Flemming
Am Fuchsengraben 1B
D-82319 Starnberg, Germany
Tel: 00 49 8151 78080
Fax: 00 49 8151 78081

Ikebana-Studio
Mr Hubert Koester
Waisenhausdamm 8-11

38100 Braunschweig, Germany
Tel: 00 49 531 43882
Fax: 00 49 531 43848

Gary McClanaham
9697 La Mora Circle
Fountain Valley
California 92708, USA
Tel: 00 1 714 964 2599
gnmcclanaham@earthlink.net

L.H. Selman Ltd
123 Locust Street
Santa Cruz
California 95060, USA
Tel: 00 1 831 427 1177
Fax: 00 1 831 427 0111
selman@paperweight.com
Website: www.paperweight.com

The Stone Gallery
93 The High Street, Burford
Oxfordshire OX18 4QA, UK
Tel & Fax: 01993 823302

Sweetbriar Gallery Ltd
Mrs A. Metcalfe
Robin Hood Lane
Helsby
Cheshire WA6 9NH, UK
Tel: 01928 723851
Fax: 01928 724153
sweetbr@globalnet.co.uk
Website: www.sweetbriar.co.uk

COLLECTORS' ASSOCIATIONS
Caithness Collectors' Club
Inveralmond
Perth PH1 3TZ, UK
Tel: 01738 492329

**Cambridge
Paperweight Circle**
56 Manor Drive North
New Malden
Surrey KT3 5NY, UK
Tel: 020 8337 7077

**Paperweight Collectors'
Association, Inc.**
Alvin Bates (President)
19302 Milestone Court
Houston, Texas 77094, USA

Perthshire Collectors' Club
14 Comrie Street, Crieff
Perthshire PH7 4AZ, UK
Tel: 017764 655151

MUSEUMS & VISITOR CENTRES
Baccarat Museum
Rue de Cristallerie
BP31 Baccarat, France
Tel: 00 33 383 766137

Bergstrom-Mahler Museum
165 North Park Avenue
Neenah, Wisconsin 54956, USA
Tel: 001 920 751 4658

Bristol Art Gallery
Queens Road
Bristol BS8 1RL, UK
Tel: 0117 922 3571

The Corning Museum of Glass
1 Museum Way
Corning, New York 14830, USA
Tel: 001 607 937 5371

Perth Museum & Art Gallery
78 George Street
Perth PH1 5LB, UK
Tel: 01738 632488

Caithness Glass Ltd
Inveralmond
Perth PH1 3TZ, UK
Tel: 01738 492320

Glyn Vivian Art Gallery
Alexandra Road, Swansea
Wales SA1 5DZ, UK
Tel: 01792 651738

Selkirk Glass
Dunsdale Haugh
Selkirk TB7 5EF, UK
Tel: 01750 20954

Index

Acknowledgments

Front jacket: Octopus Publishing Group Ltd/Stuart Chorley. All photographs © Sweetbriar Gallery, except: Caithness Glass Ltd. 9 tr; Christie's Images 20tl, 23t, 24r, 25t; Langham Glass Ltd 42b; Octopus Publishing Group Ltd/Stuart Chorley 2; Octopus Publishing Group Ltd/Steve Tanner/Sweetbriar Gallery 43l; Octopus Publishing Group Ltd/Steve Tanner/Glasform 42t; Octopus Publishing Group Ltd/Steve Tanner/Sweetbriar Gallery 13t, 16r, 19b, 21cl, 25bl, 29r, 30t, 34t, 34b, 37c, 38b, 40r, 41t, 41bl, 41br, 43c, 44l, 45b, 49c, 54l, 56l, 57c, 58b. Key: t: top, b: bottom, c: centre, l: left, r: right. The publishers would like to thank all those who contributed images for use in the book.